The Brontës

SELECTED POEMS

Edited by
JULIET R. V. BARKER

EVERYMAN
J. M. DENT · LONDON
CHARLES E. TUTTLE
VERMONT

This edition first published in Everyman by J. M. Dent 1993
Reprinted 1993
Chronology and all endmatter apart from notes
© J. M. Dent 1993

Selection, introduction and notes
© David Campbell Publishers Ltd 1985

This title first published in Everyman by J. M. Dent 1985

J. M. Dent
Orion Publishing Group
Orion House
5 Upper St Martin's Lane London, WC2H 9EA
and
Charles E. Tuttle Co. Inc.
28 South Main Street,
Rutland, Vermont 05701, USA

Typeset by Deltatype Ltd, Ellesmere Port, Cheshire.
Printed in Great Britain by
The Guernsey Press Co., Ltd, Guernsey, C.I.

British Library Cataloguing in Publication Data
is available upon request.

ISBN 0 460 87282 6

CONTENTS

POEMS BY EMILY JANE BRONTË

POEMS BY ANNE BRONTË

For James
more myself than I am

NOTES ON THE AUTHORS AND EDITOR

CHARLOTTE BRONTË was born at Thornton in 1816 but spent most her life at Haworth where her father was the parson. From childhood she wrote constantly in partnership with her brother, Branwell, progressing from stories about their shared imaginary kingdoms of Glass Town and Angria to the novels which were to make her famous. As Currer Bell she published several books. *Poems* by Currer, Ellis and Acton Bell, which she published with her sisters Emily and Anne in 1846 was a failure and her first novel, *The Professor*, rejected by many publishers, did not appear in print until after her death. Her second novel, *Jane Eyre*, was published in 1847 by Smith, Elder & Co. and won instant acclaim. *Shirley* (1849) and *Villette* (1853), also published by Smith, Elder & Co., brought her great success though they never achieved the popularity of *Jane Eyre*. She died in 1855, a few months after marrying her father's curate, Arthur Bell Nicholls.

PATRICK BRANWELL BRONTË (b.1817) was the only son of the Reverend Patrick Brontë. A talented artist and poet, Branwell tried to earn his living by painting portraits and publishing his poems, but failed. Thereafter he followed more practical careers on the Leeds and Manchester Railway and as a private tutor, but with an equal lack of success. Disillusioned and embittered by his failures, he took to alcohol and opium; he died of consumption, aged thirty-one, in 1848.

EMILY JANE BRONTË (b.1818) was the most home loving of the Brontë children and rarely left Haworth. The moors around the village were a continual source of inspiration to her and had a profound influence on her poetry and prose. In childhood she began writing stories with her younger sister, Anne, about an imaginary kingdom called Gondal – a collaboration which was to continue into adult life. Her one novel, *Wuthering Heights* (1847), sank virtually without trace during her lifetime though for the last hundred years it has been widely acknowledged as one of the greatest books in English literature. She died, aged 30, less than three months after her brother in 1848.

ANNE BRONTË (b.1820) was the youngest of the Brontë siblings and, as such, has tended to be overlooked. Quieter and less remarkable than her sisters, she was nevertheless a talented writer. Like them, she sought employment as a private governess in the households of Yorkshire country gentry but, unlike them, she managed to keep one post, at Thorp Green near York, for five years. On resigning from that position, she took up writing professionally, collaborating with Charlotte and Emily on *Poems* by Currer, Ellis and Acton Bell and then producing two novels of her own, *Agnes Grey* (1847) and *The Tenant of Wildfell Hall* (1848). Neither were successful, though *The Tenant* attracted some notoriety for its unusual subject matter, a woman leaving her debauched husband. She died in 1849, aged 29, less than six months after Emily and was buried at Scarborough, the only member of the Brontë family not to be buried at Haworth.

JULIET R. V. BARKER is an authority on the Brontës and a medieval historian. She was educated at Bradford Girls' Grammar School and St Anne's College, Oxford, where she gained a BA in History followed by a D. Phil for her thesis *The Tournament in England c.1100–1400*. For six years (1983–9) she was curator and librarian of the Brontë Parsonage Museum at Haworth, the world's largest repository of Brontë material. She has published a number of books on the Brontës and on medieval history, and appears regularly on BBC Radio 4. She is currently working on a major new biography of the Brontës.

CHRONOLOGY OF THE BRONTËS' LIVES

AB = Anne CB = Charlotte EJB = Emily PB = Patrick PBB = Branwell
My forthcoming biography of the Brontës will substantially revise several of the
hitherto accepted dates in the Brontës' lives: these revised dates are
incorporated below. JRVB

Year	Age	Brontë Chronology
1816		21 Apl: Birth of CB, third daughter of Rev Patrick and Mrs Maria Brontë, at Thornton, near Bradford, Yorkshire
1817		26 Jun: Birth of PBB, fourth child and only son
1818		PB *The Maid of Killarney*; 30 Jul: Birth of EJB, fourth daughter
1820		17 Jan: Birth of AB, sixth and last child
20 Apl: Brontë family move to Haworth on PB's appointment to the perpetual curacy
1821	38	15 Sept: Death of Mrs Maria Brontë of cancer; her elder sister, Elizabeth Branwell, moves to Haworth Parsonage to look after the Brontë family
1824		PB *The Phenomenon*
	10/9	1 Jul: Maria and Elizabeth, two eldest Brontë sisters, sent to board at the Clergy Daughters' School, Cowan Bridge, near Kirkby Lonsdale, Westmoreland
	8	10 Aug: CB joins her sisters at the Clergy Daughters' School
	6	25 Nov: EJB joins her sisters
1825	11	6 May: Death of Maria, at Haworth, of tuberculosis contracted at school
31 May: Elizabeth sent home from school dying of tuberculosis
1 Jun: PB withdraws CB and EJB from the school and brings them home

CHRONOLOGY OF THEIR TIMES

Year	Literary Context	Historical Events
1816	Walter Scott *Old Mortality*; Lord Byron Canto 1 *Childe Harold*	[Regency in Britain during madness of George III 1809–20]
1817	Death of Jane Austen; Lord Byron *Lament of Tasso*	
1818	John Keats *Endymion*	Britain becomes effective ruler of India; Peterloo massacre (1819)
1820	Percy Bysshe Shelley *Prometheus Unbound*	Death of George III; accession George IV; Cato Street conspiracy
1821	Death of John Keats; Walter Scott *Kenilworth* Death of Percy Bysshe Shelley (1822)	Greek war of independence Monroe doctrine enunciated in US (1823)
1824	Death of Lord Byron	
1825		Opening of first passenger steam railway in England, leading to railway building boom

Year	Age	Brontë Chronology
	10	15 Jun: Death of Elizabeth, at Haworth
1826		5 June: PB returns from Leeds with presents for each of the children, including the toy soldiers which inspire the creation of an imaginary world, Glasstown. The children begin to write plays, stories and poems about them in tiny hand-made books
1831	14	17 Jan: CB goes to Roe Head School, Mirfield, Yorkshire
1832	16	May: CB leaves Roe Head, having won the school prize at the end of each term; she begins to teach her sisters at home
1834	17/16	Jan: CB and PBB create a new imaginary kingdom, Angria. EJB and AB break away to found their own independent world, Gondal
1835		PB has a poem published in Leeds Mercury;
	17–18	PBB training as a professional portrait painter with view to entering the Royal Academy, a plan which was eventually abandoned;
	19/17	29 Jul: CB returns to Roe Head as a teacher, taking EJB with her as a pupil
	15	Mid Oct: EJB, unable to settle at Roe Head, returns to Haworth; her place is taken by AB
1837	17	Dec: AB falls seriously ill at Roe Head; CB, feeling AB's illness is under-estimated, resigns her post and withdraws AB from school. They return home
1838	20	May: PBB sets up as a professional portrait painter in a studio in Bradford
		Sept: EJB takes up a post as teacher in a girls' boarding school at Law Hill, Halifax
1839	21	Feb: PBB abandons his career as an artist; he returns to Haworth
	19	Apl: AB becomes governess to the Ingham family at Blake Hall, Mirfield
	23	May–Jul: CB acts as temporary governess to the Sidgwick family at Stonegappe, Lothersdale

Year	Literary Context	Historical Events
1826		Roman Catholic Relief Act (1829); accession of William IV (1830); revolutions in France, Belgium, Italy, Germany and Poland (1830)
1832	Deaths of Walter Scott and J W Goethe	Franchise extended by Reform Act (1832) Abolition of slavery in British Empire (1833)
1834	Deaths of Samuel Taylor Coleridge and Charles Lamb	Factory Act limiting employment of children (1833) Poor Law Amendment Act and trial of 'Tolpuddle Martyrs' (1834)
1837	Charles Dickens Oliver Twist	Accession of Queen Victoria; rebellion in Canada against British rule
1838		'People's Charter' demands universal male suffrage and liberalisation of parliamentary practice
1839	Harriet Martineau Deerbrook	Series of bad harvests and severe depression of trade lead to the 'hungry forties' (1839–43); Chartist National

Year	Age	Brontë Chronology
	25	Aug: William Weightman comes to Haworth as PB's curate
	19	Dec: AB dismissed from her post at Blake Hall
1840	22	Jan: PBB takes up post as tutor to Postlethwaite family at Broughton-in-Furness in the Lake District
	20	May: AB appointed governess to the Robinson family at Thorp Green, near York
	22	Jun: PBB dismissed by the Postlethwaites
	23	Oct: PBB begins work as assistant Clerk-in-Charge on the Leeds-Manchester railway at Sowerby Bridge station near Halifax
1841	24	Mar: CB appointed governess to the White family at Upperwood House, Rawdon, near Leeds
	23	Apl: PBB promoted to Clerk-in-Charge at Luddendenfoot station near Sowerby Bridge
	23	5 Jun: The *Halifax Guardian* publishes the first of twelve poems by PBB
	25	Dec: CB resigns her post at Upperwood House
1842		PBB has six poems published in the *Halifax Guardian*, eight in the *Bradford Herald* and one in
	64/25/23	the *Leeds Mercury*; 8 Feb: PB escorts CB and EJB to Brussels where they enter the Pensionnat Heger as boarding pupils
	24	31 Mar: PBB dismissed from the Leeds-Manchester railway for failing to keep proper accounts
	28	6 Sept: Death of Rev William Weightman, curate of Haworth, from cholera
	66	29 Oct: Death of 'Aunt' Elizabeth Branwell
	26/24	5 Nov: CB and EJB leave Brussels for home on hearing of Aunt Branwell's illness and death
1843	26	27 Jan: CB returns alone to Brussels to combine her studies with teaching duties at the Pensionnat Heger
1844	27	1 Jan: CB finally leaves Brussels with a diploma from Monsieur Heger with whom she has fallen in love

Year	Literary Context	Historical Events
1840		Convention leads to riots and strikes; Britain annexes New Zealand; First postage stamps issued; Union of Upper and Lower Canada
1841	Robert Browning *Bells and Pomegranates*; H W Longfellow *Ballads and Other Poems*	Robert Peel Prime Minister (1841–6)
1843	Death of Robert Southey	
1844		Second railway boom (1844–7)

Year	Age	Brontë Chronology
		July-Oct: plans for the sisters to set up a boarding school at the parsonage revived but abandoned when no pupils can be found
1845		PBB has four poems published in the *Yorkshire Gazette* and two in the *Halifax Guardian*;
	26	25 May: Rev Arthur Bell Nicholls comes to Haworth as curate to PB
	25	11 Jun: AB resigns her post at Thorp Green and returns home
	28	Jul: PBB dismissed from Thorp Green when his liaison with Mrs Robinson is discovered
	29	Oct: CB discovers a manuscript book of EJB's poems and persuades her sisters to publish a joint collection of their poems; they also each begin to write a novel with a view to publication
1846		PBB and EJB each have a poem published in the *Halifax Guardian*; May: Publication of *Poems* by Currer, Ellis and Acton Bell by Aylott & Jones: despite some good reviews only two copies are sold
	30	25 Aug: CB begins second novel, *Jane Eyre*, while nursing her father after an operation for the removal of cataracts in Manchester
1847	27	Jun: AB completes her second novel, *The Tenant of Wildfell Hall*; PBB last poem published in the *Halifax Guardian*
	28/27	Jul: T C Newby accepts EJB's *Wuthering Heights* and AB's *Agnes Grey* for publication but rejects CB's first novel, *The Professor*
	31	Aug: Smith, Elder & Co reject *The Professor* but accept *Jane Eyre*
	31	16 Oct: Publication of *Jane Eyre* to instant success; three editions printed in six months
	29/27	Dec: Publication of *Wuthering Heights* and *Agnes Grey*; Newby suggests they are by Currer Bell
1848	28/32	Jul: Publication, by Newby, of AB's *The Tenant of Wildfell Hall*. CB and AB go to London to prove their separate identities

Year	Literary Context	Historical Events
1845		Irish famine; US annexes Texas; J H Newman, founder of Oxford movement, becomes a Roman Catholic
1846		Britain repeals corn laws; Mexican war begins.
1847	W M Thackeray *Vanity Fair* (1847–8)	Factory Act limits children and women to ten-hour working day
1848	Mrs Gaskell *Mary Barton*; Marx and Engels *Communist Manifesto*	'Year of Revolution' in Europe; proclamation of Third Republic in France

Year	Age	Brontë Chronology
	31	24 Sept: Death of PBB from tuberculosis Nov: Re-issue of *Poems* by Currer, Ellis & Acton Bell by Smith, Elder & Co
	30	19 Dec: Death of EJB from tuberculosis; AB poem in *Fraser's Magazine* and *Leeds Intelligencer*
1849	29	28 May: Death of AB from tuberculosis, at Scarborough where she is buried in St Mary's churchyard
	33	28 Aug: CB completes her third novel, *Shirley* 26 Oct: Publication of *Shirley*; CB's true identity begins to be known Dec: CB stays with George Smith, of Smith, Elder & Co in London, meeting W M Thackeray and Harriet Martineau
1850		CB has a poem published in the *Manchester Athenaeum Album*; May-Jul: CB stays with the
	34	Smiths in London, sits for her portrait to George Richmond then travels to Edinburgh with the Smiths Aug: CB meets Mrs Gaskell while staying in the Lake District 10 Dec: Smith, Elder & Co publish a single volume edition of *Wuthering Heights* and *Agnes Grey* with a biographical preface by CB
1851		Apl: James Taylor of Smith, Elder & Co, proposes to CB but is refused and goes to India
	35	May-Jun: CB stays with Smiths in London, going to Thackeray's lectures, the theatre and the Great Exhibition; she then visits Mrs Gaskell in Manchester Nov: CB begins her fourth novel, *Villette*, but is delayed by serious ill-health
1852	36	Nov: CB sends completed manuscript of *Villette* to Smith, Elder & Co
	33	13 Dec: Rev Arthur Bell Nicholls proposes to Charlotte but is refused by her at her father's insistence
1853	36	Jan-Feb: CB stays with Smiths in London for a month for publication of *Villette*

Year	Literary Context	Historical Events
1849	Charles Dickens *David Copperfield;* death of Hartley Coleridge	
1850	Death of William Wordsworth; Elizabeth Barrett Browning *Sonnets from the Portuguese*	Death of Robert Peel
1851	John Ruskin *The Stones of Venice* (1851–3)	Great Exhibition in London
1852	Harriet Beecher Stowe *Uncle Tom's Cabin*	Fall of French Republic, Napoleon III becomes emperor
1853	Mrs Gaskell *Ruth*	Livingstone begins African explorations. Factory Act extends ten-hour working day to men

Year	Age	Brontë Chronology
	37	Apl: CB visits Mrs Gaskell in Manchester
	34	May: Arthur Bell Nicholls leaves Haworth to become curate of Kirk Smeaton near Pontefract
		Sept: Mrs Gaskell stays with Charlotte at Haworth
1854	37/35	Apl: CB becomes officially engaged to Arthur Bell Nicholls, her father having withdrawn his opposition to the match
		May: CB visits Mrs Gaskell in Manchester
	38/35	29 Jun: CB marries Arthur Bell Nicholls in Haworth church; they spend their honeymoon in Ireland then return to live with PB at Haworth Parsonage
1855	39	31 Mar: CB dies in the early stages of pregnancy
		Jul: PB asks Mrs Gaskell to write CB's biography
1857		25 Mar: Publication by Smith, Elder & Co of Mrs Gaskell's Life of CB
		6 Jun: First publication of The Professor, CB's first novel, by Smith, Elder & Co
1860		Apl: CB's last, unfinished novel, Emma, published in The Cornhill Magazine with a preface by Thackeray
1861	84/42	7 Jun: Death of PB; Arthur Bell Nicholls retires from church and returns to Ireland
1864	45	25 Aug: Arthur Bell Nicholls marries his cousin Mary Bell
1906	87	2 Dec: Death of Arthur Bell Nicholls at Banagher in Ireland

Year	Literary Context	Historical Events
1854	Charles Dickens *Hard Times*	Crimean War begins; Florence Nightingale goes to nurse in the Crimea; Oxford and Cambridge opened up to dissenters from Church of England
1855		Treaty of Paris ends Crimean War (1856)
1857	Anthony Trollope *Barchester Towers*; Charles Darwin *The Origin of the Species* (1859)	Indian mutiny
1860	George Eliot *The Mill on the Floss*; Wilkie Collins *The Woman in White*; Charles Dickens *Great Expectations*	
1861	Death of Elizabeth Barrett Browning	Death of Prince Albert; American Civil War begins

PREFACE

I was prompted to make this selection of poems by the numerous inquiries I have received for a readily available and reasonably priced edition of the best-known Brontë poems. I have therefore chosen the popular poems which are most often requested, those generally acknowledged to be the best and those, perhaps less well known, which I consider deserve to reach a wider audience. Those who wish to go on to a more comprehensive knowledge of the complete range of poetry produced by the Brontës, developing from the comparatively crude early writings, or to detailed textual criticism, can turn to the scholarly complete editions which are either available or in preparation. I have added a few notes on each poem giving first the date of composition; secondly the context, whether biographical or fictional; and thirdly more detailed comments on the text where appropriate.

For the poems of Charlotte and Anne, I have used the texts printed by Clement Shorter in *The Complete Poems of Charlotte Brontë* and *The Complete Poems of Anne Brontë*, both published by Hodder & Stoughton in 1923, except for no. 87, for which I have preferred the fuller text taken from the manuscript printed in Brontë Society *Transactions* 8:42:22–4. For Emily's, I have used C.W. Hatfield, *The Complete Poems of Emily Jane Brontë* (Columbia University Press, 1941). Hatfield worked from manuscript sources in preference to printed texts. Where a poem was included in the 1846 or 1850 editions prepared by the sisters themselves, the notes indicate whether the text printed here is the same as or differs from the 1846 or 1850 texts. The texts of Branwell's poems are taken from various sources: nos. 21 and 22 are from John Drinkwater's *The Odes of Quintus Horatius Flaccus Book I Translated by Patrick Branwell Brontë* (privately printed, 1923); nos. 23 and 25 are from Brontë Society *Transac-*

tions 7:37, pp.88–90 and 74–82 respectively; no. 24 is from F.H.
Grundy, *Pictures of the Past* (Griffith & Farran, 1879), pp.78–9;
no. 26 is from F.A. Leyland, *The Brontë Family* (Hurst &
Blackett, 1886), i, 300; no. 19 is published in facsimile in C.K.
Shorter, *The Complete Works of Emily Jane Brontë* (Hodder &
Stoughton, 1910), i (Prose), 446, where it is wrongly attributed
to Emily; and nos. 16, 17, 18 and 20 are from the Hatfield
Transcripts in the archives of the Brontë Parsonage Museum at
Haworth.

INTRODUCTION

The Brontës

The story of the Brontës has been written many times and yet there are very few, if any, satisfactory biographies. A romantic tradition, even legend, has grown up around the family, chiefly because the work of biography has often fallen into the hands of novelists, attracted by the undoubtedly tragic events in the Brontës lives, the moments of high drama and the supposedly doom-laden atmosphere of Haworth Parsonage where 'every movement, even to the flicker of their eyelids, was fatal and ominous' (E. & G. Romieu, *The Brontë Sisters,* London, 1931, p.253). The very first biography, Mrs Gaskell's *Life of Charlotte Brontë*, published in 1857 (two years after Charlotte's death) is a popular work and a classic in its own right. Nevertheless, it is a highly coloured account; Mrs Gaskell deliberately set out (with the best intentions) to lionise Charlotte and turn her into a heroine worthy of romantic fiction; a heroine who had struggled for years against all the disadvantages of ill-health, physical isolation and lack of money eventually to win fame, if not fortune, in the literary world. Most later biographers have unquestioningly accepted Mrs Gaskell's views as facts, thereby perpetuating some of the more popular misconceptions about the Brontës.

One of Mrs Gaskell's victims was the Reverend Patrick Brontë; an elderly chronic invalid by the time she met him, he was embittered by the loss of all his children and she felt unable to question him too closely. She therefore went for information to the villagers of Haworth and so produced a caricature of the man which could hardly be further from the truth.

Patrick Brontë was born in 1777 in a tiny cottage in Ireland. His father was a farmer and, as the eldest of ten children, he was expected to earn his own living at an early age. He may have spent some time as a weaver, but personal ambition led him to teach himself to read and write to such a standard that he became the village schoolmaster at sixteen and at twenty-five he entered St John's College, Cambridge. Four years later, he was ordained in the Church of England and took up a series of curacies which eventually brought him to the West Riding of Yorkshire. It was while he was vicar of Hartshead, near Huddersfield, that he met Maria Branwell, the daughter of a prosperous merchant from Penzance in Cornwall, who was visiting relatives at Woodhouse Grove School near Bradford, where Patrick was an examiner in the Classics. After a rapid courtship they were married on 29 December 1812 in an unusual double wedding ceremony with Maria's cousin, Jane Fennell, and Patrick's friend William Morgan.

Eight years later Mr Brontë was appointed to St Michael and All Angels Church, Haworth, his last and longest appointment. The parish, though rural and remote by today's standards, was an important one spiritually for it was here that the Reverend William Grimshaw, an early disciple of Wesley, had ministered. It was therefore with a sense of excitement that Mr and Mrs Brontë came to Haworth with their young family. By this time there were six children: Maria (b. 1814), Elizabeth (b. 1815), Charlotte (b. 1816), Patrick Branwell, known as Branwell, the only son (b. 1817), Emily Jane (b. 1818) and Anne (b. 1820).

The Parsonage (now a museum) was at the top of the steep cobbled main street, on the outskirts of the village but also on the edge of large tracts of open moorland. This position was of central importance in the Brontës' lives: the family had few friends in the village, where most of the men, women and even children worked in the woollen industry. The young Brontës therefore had to fashion their own entertainment amongst themselves: on the other hand, they had the freedom of the moors where they could range at will. Even as small children the Brontës were avid walkers and it was not long before all the moorland paths, streams and valleys round their new home were known to them.

Within eighteen months of moving to Haworth, Mrs Brontë died. Patrick had little or no chance of marrying again and it was fortunate, therefore, that Elizabeth Branwell, Mrs Brontë's sister, was prepared to leave her home in Penzance and take charge of the young family at Haworth. A spinster who had been the belle of the Assembly Rooms in Penzance, Aunt Branwell became a figure of fun to the children with her old-fashioned ways and her little eccentricities: she was also a remarkably intelligent woman who could hold her own against Mr Brontë in political arguments and an authoritarian who imposed some much-needed discipline on the wild and wayward children for which Charlotte, at least, was grateful in later life.

In July 1824 Maria and Elizabeth, the two eldest daughters, were sent away to school for the first time, followed by Charlotte and Emily. The Clergy Daughters' School at Cowan Bridge was a charitable institution intended to provide an education for the daughters of impoverished clergymen who would not otherwise have been able to afford it. The school was in its infancy and its founder and director, the Reverend William Carus Wilson, was a strict disciplinarian whose harsh regime and moralistic attitudes were calculated to upset the sensitive Brontë girls, who were not in robust health. The following spring both Maria and Elizabeth had to be removed owing to ill-health; on 6 May 1825 Maria died, aged eleven, and on 15 June Elizabeth died, aged ten, both from consumption, their constitutions fatally weakened by their time at Cowan Bridge. In the meantime Charlotte and Emily had been brought back to Haworth, but the catastrophic events of these months were to leave a permanent scar on the children, particularly Charlotte, who was now to take over her beloved eldest sister's role as mother to the family; many years later she poured out her bitterness in her description of Lowood School in *Jane Eyre*.

For six years no attempt was made to send the children away to school again. Aunt Branwell's temporary residence became permanent and the girls were given their lessons in household duties by her and shared Branwell's academic lessons with their father. They read voraciously and indiscriminately, ranging from the Scottish border ballads and novels of Walter Scott through to the political journals of the day, such as *Blackwood's Magazine*. Their education was unconventional but nonetheless stimulating.

In 1826, Mr Brontë bought Branwell a box of toy wooden soldiers; when the box was opened, the children each chose their own particular soldier, gave him a name and a character and began to write stories about him set in an imaginary kingdom. Thus began the great Glasstown sagas which were to dominate their imaginative lives for the next twenty years. The stories, carefully written in minute script intended to resemble bookprint, were made up into little books no bigger than a matchbox which were just large enough for a toy soldier to hold in his hands. Originally a collaboration between the four children, the stories began to take different directions when Emily and Anne split away and formed their own kingdom with their own characters. Charlotte and Branwell turned to write about Angria, a new kingdom conquered out of the African wilderness surrounding Glasstown, while Emily and Anne turned to Gondal, an island in the South Pacific. The characters of Angria and Gondal quickly became mouthpieces for a positive flood of writing, providing an outlet for all the emotions and frustrations of the Brontës' lives. Most of the writing was prose, but at suitable dramatic moments poetry was used to highlight emotional intensity and much of the Brontës' poetry belongs to this imaginary world rather than to personal experience.

In 1831 Charlotte went, of her own volition, to Roe Head school at Mirfield, realising that she needed to have formal schooling and paper qualifications if she was ever to be able to earn her own living – as was essential if she did not marry, since Mr Brontë's house and income were tied to his employment and on his death the children would be left homeless and virtually penniless. The choice of school was much better this time: the principal, Miss Wooler, was enlightened and encouraging and under her influence the school (and Charlotte) flourished. There Charlotte made several life-long friends, including Ellen Nussey and Mary Taylor, her fellow pupils, and Miss Wooler herself. When she left school she carried off the silver medal for achievement and Miss Wooler invited her back as a governess with one of her sisters as a free pupil. Emily, as the next eldest, was chosen, but after only two months she was so ill with homesickness that she left and her place was taken by Anne, who proved more adaptable.

At this period, the Brontës harboured ambitions to be poets; their father had set them a shining example in this field for he was the proud author of several books of poetry and prose as well as a regular contributor to the local press. No doubt this was one of the reasons for their aspirations to appear in print and both Charlotte and Branwell took practical steps to emulate him. In 1837 Charlotte wrote to the Poet Laureate, Robert Southey, enclosing copies of some of her verses and asking for his opinion of her talents. This brought a discouraging reply advising her that literature could not be and should not be the business of a woman's life and suggesting that she should write poetry solely for its own sake and not with a view to earning fame by it. The one consolation was Southey's comment: 'You evidently possess, and in no inconsiderable degree, what Wordsworth calls the "faculty of verse".' (L. & L., i, 127.) Charlotte evidently took this opinion to heart, for she preserved the letter, writing upon the envelope, 'Southey's advice to be kept for ever. My twenty-first birthday. Roe Head, April 21, 1837.'

While Charlotte was writing to Southey, Branwell was writing to William Wordsworth, though his bombastic tone and comments such as, 'there is not a *writing* poet worth a sixpence' (L. & L., i, 136), were not calculated to appeal and he received no reply. He did not lose heart, however, and in 1840, having met Hartley Coleridge during a visit to the Lakes, he sent him his translation of the first book of Horace's *Odes*, hoping that it might be possible for him to earn a living as a translator of the classics. The translation was more than competent (see nos. 21 and 22) but did not attract publication until long after Branwell's death. Though many of his own compositions found their way into print in local newspapers, Branwell was forced to accept that he could not earn a living by the pen.

In 1838, the Brontës were all attempting to earn their own livings. Branwell, who had shown considerable talent as an artist and had received lessons from the professional Leeds-based portrait painter William Robinson, himself a pupil of Sir Thomas

Lawrence, set up a portrait-painting studio in Bradford; Charlotte had left Miss Wooler's school and gone to take up a private post as a governess in Lothersdale, Emily spent six months as a teacher at Law Hill near Halifax and Anne, the following year, also became a private governess in Mirfield. All these posts were of short duration: Branwell returned home in debt in February 1839, became a private tutor at Broughton-in-Furness for six months in 1840 and then joined the new Halifax railway, initially as a clerk, though he was soon promoted to become station-master at Luddenden Foot; Charlotte spent only two months at Lothersdale, followed by a spell of less than a year as a governess at Rawdon in 1841; Emily did not attempt to seek employment again, preferring to remain at home as housekeeper while Anne, after nine months at Mirfield, found another post with the Robinsons of Thorp Green near York.

As the rapid changes of these years suggest, none of the Brontës was temperamentally suited to teaching, resenting the restrictions on their pirvacy and the demands on their time which private tutorial work necessarily involved. However, as daughters of a clergyman, they had no other socially acceptable career open to them. The alternative to being private governesses was to begin a school of their own where at least they could retain a modicum of control over their own lives. In 1842, as a step towards fulfilling this ambition, Charlotte and Emily went to Brussels to become pupils at the Pensionnat Heger, a boarding school for Belgian girls which took a few foreign pupils. The idea for this surprisingly adventurous move came from Charlotte's schoolfriend, Mary Taylor, who was already enjoying a Continental education in a more expensive Brussels school. The finance was provided by Aunt Branwell, who advanced some of the money she had intended to leave as legacies to the girls in response to a passionately worded appeal from Charlotte: 'Papa will perhaps think it a wild and ambitious scheme; but who ever rose in the world without ambition? When he left Ireland to go to Cambridge University, he was as ambitious as I am now. I want us *all* to go on. I know we have talents, and I want them to be turned to account.' (L. & L., i, 221.)

Life in a Brussels school was a revelation. Both girls were homesick but this time even Emily fought back and her 'indomitable will' conquered her feelings. They used their time to the best advantage, knowing it would be of short duration, making special studies of French and German and, in the case of Emily, developing a remarkable talent for music under the aegis of one of the best professors Belgium could provide. The avidity with which they studied, as well as their foreign ways and ostentatious Protestantism, set them apart from the other, much younger, pupils but they attracted the attention of Monsieur Heger, husband of the principal of the school. Monsieur Heger was himself an unconventional man who used unusual teaching methods to which the Brontë girls, at first bewildered, responded eagerly. Their French improved under his guidance but he also encouraged and nurtured their creative gifts; his praise, sparingly given, was a reward worth striving for and Charlotte especially returned his admiration of their intellectual powers with a hero-worship that became increasingly fanatical. The six months originally planned was extended to a year, but this was cut short when news reached them that Aunt Branwell was seriously ill. Before they could even pack their bags, they heard that she had died and they returned home immediately to find the Parsonage in chaos. Mr Brontë no longer had his housekeeper and Branwell was almost unhinged by the double loss inside a month of his best friend, the curate William Weightman, and his aunt to whom he had been very close.

Emily gratefully seized the chance of remaining at home to keep house for Mr Brontë, leaving Charlotte free to return to Brussels. Anne went back to Thorp Green, this time taking Branwell with her as a tutor for the young Robinson boy who had outgrown her care. In the new year, Charlotte made her way back to Brussels alone where, without her sister's companionship, she became more dependent than ever upon Monsieur Heger and almost obsessional about winning his approval. After a year of mental torture, she decided to leave and returned to Haworth sick in heart and mind, despite having achieved her initial object of acquiring further qualifications for teaching.

Once again the plan for setting up a school for young ladies at Haworth Parsonage was revived; circulars were printed advertising their terms (£35 per annum) and these were distributed among their friends and acquaintances. They received not a single inquiry and the long-cherished plan had finally to be laid to rest.

In June 1845 Anne suddenly resigned her post at Thorp Green and one month later she was followed home by Branwell. The whole sorry story soon emerged, though its details were hidden in half-truths and deliberate lies. Branwell had conceived an ill-advised passion for his employer's wife: whether or not she encouraged him, his family believed that she was the prime mover in the affair. The Brontës' servants later told how the two had been caught together in the boat sheds at Thorp Green by one of the gardeners who told Mr Robinson and Branwell was summarily dismissed. From that time Branwell became a terrible trial to his family: already a heavy drinker he became an alcoholic and possibly an opium-eater (though the addiction caused by opium was not yet recognised in an age where the drug was widely available as a pain killer and administered even to children). He refused to find further employment, blackmailed and stole from his father to obtain money for his drink and drugs, and became violent and unpredictable.

Given Branwell's condition and the fact that he was already widely published in local newspapers, it is not surprising that the sisters did not include him in their next project – the publication in May 1846 of a slim volume of *Poems* by Currer, Ellis and Acton Bell. The pseudonyms were chosen deliberately to veil the sex of the poets, since the Brontës were determined to be judged on their work alone and not lay themselves open to reviewers' criticism on the grounds of their sex. The idea for the book arose when Charlotte accidentally discovered a manuscript book of Emily's poetry; on reading it through, 'something more than surprise seized me – a deep conviction that these were not common effusions, nor at all like the poetry women generally write. I thought them condensed and terse, vigorous and genuine. To my ear they had also a peculiar music, wild, melancholy, and elevating.' (L. & L., i, 317.)

Emily was furious to find that her privacy had been violated, and it took some days of persuasion and Anne's offering of her own poems before Emily was placated enough to agree to allow a selection of her work to be published. Since all the sisters (and Branwell) had continued writing the histories of Angria and Gondal from childhood, most of their poetry had its origins in these imaginary kingdoms and it was therefore necessary, when preparing for publication, to re-edit the poems and obfuscate any references which might lead the public to suspect their private worlds. The book was published at the sisters' own expense by Aylott and Jones of London: it cost them in the region of £50, including printing and advertising, a sum which was provided out of legacies from Aunt Branwell. Only two copies of the book were sold, but it received some favourable reviews which encouraged the sisters not to give up hope.

They therefore turned their attention to prose and this time deliberately set out to write novels for the popular market. Charlotte wrote *The Professor*, an exploration of the type of pupil-teacher relationship which she herself had enjoyed with Monsieur Heger in Brussels; Anne wrote *Agnes Grey*, based on the life of a governess; and Emily wrote *Wuthering Heights* which was, in many ways, simply an extension of the Gondal world. The completed manuscripts were hawked around the publishers until *Wuthering Heights* and *Agnes Grey* were accepted by Thomas Newby; *The Professor* did not find a publisher until after Charlotte's death, but when she accompanied her father to Manchester for a cataract operation on his eyes in August 1846 she began to write *Jane Eyre*. The book was written quickly, accepted immediately by Smith, Elder and Co. and published in October 1847, before Newby had even published her sisters' novels. When *Jane Eyre* brought instant fame to Currer Bell, Newby rushed through publication of *Wuthering Heights* and *Agnes Grey*, realising that Ellis and Acton Bell had some connection with Currer, but these received little critical attention except in connection with *Jane Eyre*. When the unscrupulous Newby tried to pass off his American editions as the earlier works of Currer Bell, Charlotte and Anne travelled to London to reveal their true and separate identities to Smith, Elder and Co. In the same month (July 1848) Newby published Anne's second novel, *The Tenant of Wildfell Hall*. Perhaps surprisingly, Emily did not offer another manuscript at the same time, though Anne's second novel filled three volumes in its own right and did not require any additional material on this occasion (*Agnes Grey* had filled one volume and *Wuthering Heights* two volumes of the three-volume set in which novels were published at this time).

On 24 September 1848 Branwell Brontë died suddenly, his constitution ruined by addiction to alcohol and drugs which made him vulnerable to the family disease, consumption. The shock of his death had barely registered when Emily too fell ill: she had caught a cold at Branwell's funeral and was unable to shake it off. She grew gradually weaker, coughing persistently but utterly refusing to consult a doctor or take any medication except Locock's cough wafers.

At about two o'clock in the afternoon of 19 December 1848 Emily died on the sofa in the Parsonage dining room, too weak to climb the stairs to bed. Her terrible fight for life, described by Charlotte as the 'conflict of the strangely strong spirit and the fragile frame . . . relentless conflict – once seen, never to be forgotten' (L. & L., ii, 16), nearly broke her sisters' hearts. Even then, their troubles were not at an end: Anne was to be the next victim of consumption. Her decline was more gradual than that of Emily and there was some comfort in her willingness to submit to the blisters and medication prescribed by doctors in the vain hope of restoring her health. In May, Anne and Charlotte travelled to Scarborough with Ellen Nussey to try a sea cure and it was there that Anne died on 28 May 1849; the two friends buried her in St Mary's churchyard, under the castle and overlooking the sea she had always loved, to save Mr Brontë the trauma of burying his third child in the space of nine months.

Charlotte returned home desolate and threw herself into her work, completing her third novel, *Shirley*, which had been begun before Branwell's death. It was published in October 1849 and the critics were, on the whole, kind, praising its power and cleverness. Her publishers invited her to London and now her real identity, which she had managed to keep hidden behind the psudonym Currer Bell, gradually became known. She was invited to several parties where she was introduced to two of her great literary heroes, William Makepeace Thackeray and Harriet Martineau. From this time on she took her place in London literary circles where she was lionised, not least because of her unconventional attributes – her tiny person, her provincialism and her shyness. She visited not only London, but also Edinburgh with George Smith of Smith, Elder and Co., Harriet Martineau at Windermere and Mrs Gaskell in Manchester. In December 1852 she published her fourth and last novel, *Villette*, a reworking of her Brussels experiences, which again received much critical acclaim.

The same month, the Reverend Arthur Bell Nicholls, her father's curate for the past seven years, proposed marriage to her. She was taken completely by surprise, but the hostility which the proposal (the fourth she had received) aroused in her father, the servants and their acquaintances caused Charlotte to feel some unexpected sympathy with her suitor. His persistence, unconcealed admiration and evident unhappiness gradually won her respect and approval and by April 1854 she had entered an engagement with him.

They were married in Haworth Church on 29 June 1854. Ellen Nussey was her bridesmaid and Miss Wooler gave her away, as her father felt unable to attend at the last minute. They honeymooned in Ireland, the land of her father's and her husband's birth, and Charlotte found herself unexpectedly and unbelievably happy, discovering in her husband's love and protective attitude a sense of security and fulfilment she had never known before. Nine brief months later she was dead, physically worn out by the strain of pregnancy, before she could give birth to her first child. She was thirty-eight years old.

Mr Brontë outlived all his children, surviving to the great age of eighty-four and dying six years after his last child. On his death in 1861, Mr Nicholls left Haworth Parsonage, where he had stayed to nurse his father-in-law, and returned to his native Ireland where he died in 1906, thus severing the last remaining direct link with the Brontës of Haworth.

The Poems

The Brontës are famous as novelists but they all began their literary careers as poets. As we have seen, Charlotte and Branwell both had ambitions to earn their livings as poets and sought professional advice on their work from Southey, Wordsworth, and Hartley Coleridge. Even Charlotte, who was the poorest poet of the four, won Southey's praise for her 'faculty of verse'. This was a fair assessment for much of Charlotte's work is 'verse' rather than 'poetry': her strict adherence to the rules of rhythm and metre and even more to the rhyme patterns she set herself tended to cramp her poetic expression. Often her attempts to rhyme are frankly risible, reducing much of her juvenile poetry to the level of doggerel. In her later years, however, as her style became less flowery and more natural and she became capable of making her rhyme schemes less obtrusive, she wrote some fine and memorable poetry, particularly when inspired to write by personal experience rather than by the vicarious experiences of her Angrian characters. Even so, she was much more at ease in prose and it is in the novels that her best and most lyrical writing is to be found.

Branwell's poetry is altogether in a different class. Like Charlotte, his obsession with the melodramatic world of Angria coloured his earlier poems with a hyperbole and affectation which hindered the development of his poetic instincts. In his late teens, however, he acquired a much sparer and more disciplined style, perhaps as a result of his study of classical poetry. This gave a new dimension to his work and, like Emily, he found that a terse, compressed use of words was a more effective way of capturing a powerful and emotional atmosphere than mere verbosity. His brilliant vignettes in which he deftly sets the scene reveal him to have been as acute an observer of the natural world as Emily, though it is human lives and human affairs which inspire most of his poetry. For Branwell, Angria continued to be a fertile source of character and situation, suitable for poetic exploration, until the end of his life, but his personal poetry is equally powerful. The latter is interesting, too, in that it gives us an added dimension, charting the course of his early hopes and aspirations, as he looked for models to the great figures (particularly literary figures) of the past, through to bitter disappointment and his subsequent disillusionment. At his best Branwell easily rivals Emily as a poet, giving a tantalising glimpse of talents which could have produced a novel of the calibre of *Wuthering Heights* had they been rightly channelled and developed. Branwell is not only the most underestimated member of the Brontë family but also one of the most underrated of English poets.

Emily, on the other hand, is the only Brontë to be equally well known for her prose and poetry and she rightly holds one of the first places in the pantheon of English poets. Her work occupies a disproportionately large part of this anthology, but it is a disproportion based on quality. Though the bulk of her poetry belongs to the world of Gondal, it still stands on its own and is capable of being read and enjoyed without any conception of the vast and complex imaginative world which lies behind it, unlike much of Charlotte and Branwell's Angrian verse. An understanding of the Gondal background is helpful, however, for it makes clear that many of the more extreme misanthropic and defiant sentiments are spoken through Gondal characters rather than being Emily's own personal beliefs. This is particularly important in that biographers have looked to her poetry to fill the almost total lack of autobiographical material in Emily's life. Emily's poetry is a celebration of the natural world and the powers of the imagination. Her style is terse and deceptively simple: elegiac in its sombre moods, apocalyptic in its exultant moods. The atmosphere is invariably highly charged with emotion, for the sight of wild flowers or bleak moorlands could arouse in her as poignant an emotion as could the deepest human sufferings.

Emily's pantheistic worship of nature and idolatrous worship of imagination are in stark contrast to the quiet Christianity which permeates Anne's poetry. Although she shared her sister's passion for nature and Gondal, this did not dominate her life in the way that it did the shockingly unorthodox Emily. God was at the centre of Anne's soul and even in her darkest moments when she doubted her own salvation she did not doubt His existence.

Anne's poetry frequently contains a pathos, lacking in her brother's and sisters' work, which is partly the result of her striving to attain a Christian resignation in the face of the promptings of her wilful heart. For this reason, much of her best poetry was written during her unhappy five years as a governess at Thorp Green when she was trying to reconcile her duty with her feelings. Anne's style, like Emily's, is simple and uncomplicated and there are many echoes in form, in subject matter and in treatment of her Gondal partner's poetry.

The Brontës deserve to be read as poets in their own right, not simply as novelists who also wrote poetry. They were all good poets and Emily and Branwell were excellent ones. Their close collaboration in writing and the resultant interdependence of their work makes it important for their poems to be read together and not in isolation, for, after all, one of the most remarkable things about the Brontës was that one family produced four such talented writers.

JULIET R. V. BARKER

POEMS BY
CHARLOTTE BRONTË

1 *Lines on Seeing the Portrait of . . .*
   Painted by De Lisle

    Radiant creature! is thy birth
    Of the heavens or of the earth?
    For those bright and beaming eyes
    Speak the language of the skies;
5   And, methinks, upon thy tongue
    Dwell the songs by angels sung!
    Still and tranquil is the beam
    That from those blue orbs doth stream, –
    Like the azure moon-lit sky,
10   Like the lucid stars on high, –
    Rays of mind are darting thence
    Mild and pure intelligence.

    Art though then of spirit birth
    And not a denizen of earth?
15   No! thou'rt but a child of clay,
    Simply robed in white array;
    Not a gem is gleaming there;
    All as spotless snow so fair,
    Symbol of thy angel-mind –
20   Meek, benevolent, and kind;
    Sprightly as the beauteous fawn
    Springing up at break of dawn,
    Graceful, bounding o'er the hills
    To the music of the rills!

25   What bright hues thy cheeks adorn
    Like the blushes of the morn!

How thy curled and glossy hair
Clusters o'er thy forehead fair!
How the sportive ringlets deck
30   Like golden snow thy ivory neck!
And thy hands so smooth and white
Folded, while the rosy light
Of a summer sunset sky
Gleams around thee gloriously,
35   All the west one crimson flood
Pouring light o'er mount and wood!

Beauteous being, most divine!
I am thine, and thou art mine!

2 Marion's Song

He is gone, and all grandeur has fled from the mountain;
All beauty departed from stream and from fountain;
A dark veil is hung
O'er the bright sky of gladness;
5   And where birds sweetly sung
There's a murmur of sadness.
The wind sings with a warning tone
Through many a shadowy tree;
I hear, in every passing moan,
10   The voice of destiny.

Then, O Lord of the waters! the Great! and All-seeing!
Preserve, in Thy mercy, his safety and being;
May he trust in Thy might
When the dark storm is howling,
15   And the blackness of night
Over heaven is scowling.
But may the sea flow glidingly
With gentle summer waves;
And silent may all tempests lie
20   Chained in Aeolian caves!

Yet, though ere he returnest, long years will have
    vanished,
Sweet hope from my bosom shall never be banished:
      I will think of the time
    When his step, lightly bounding,
25   Shall be heard on the rock
    Where the cataract is sounding:
When the banner of his father's host
    Shall be unfurled on high
To welcome back the pride and boast
30   Of England's chivalry!

Yet tears will flow forth while of hope I am singing;
Still Despair her dark shadow is over me flinging;
      But when he's far away,
    I will pluck the wild flower
35   On bank and on brae
    At the still, moonlight hour;
And I will twine for him a wreath
    Low in the fairies' dell;
Methought I heard the night-wind breathe
40   That solemn word, 'Farewell!'

3 *Lines on Bewick*

The cloud of recent death is past away,
    But yet a shadow lingers o'er his tomb
To tell that the pale standard of decay
    Is reared triumphant o'er life's sullied bloom.

5   But now the eye bedimmed by tears may gaze
    On the fair lines his gifted pencil drew,
The tongue unfaltering speak its meed of praise
    When we behold those scenes to Nature true –

True to the common Nature that we see
10   In England's sunny fields, her hills and vales,

On the wild bosom of her storm-dark sea
    Still heaving to the wind that o'er it wails.

How many winged inhabitants of air,
    How many plume-clad floaters of the deep,
15 The mighty artist drew in forms as fair
    As those that now the skies and waters sweep;

From the great eagle, with his lightning eye,
    His tyrant glance, his talons dyed in blood,
To the sweet breather-forth of melody,
20   The gentle merry minstrel of the wood.

Each in his attitude of native grace
    Looks on the grazer life-like, free and bold,
And if the rocks be his abiding place
    Far off appears the winged marauder's hold.

25 But if the little builder rears his nest
    In the still shadow of green tranquil trees,
And singing sweetly 'mid the silence blest
    Sits a meet emblem of untroubled peace,

'A change comes o'er the spirit of our dream,' –
30 Woods wave around in crested majesty;
We almost feel the joyous sunshine's beam
    And hear the breath of the sweet south go by.

Our childhood's days return again in thought,
    We wander in a land of love and light,
35 And mingled memories, joy – and sorrow – fraught
    Gush on our hearts with overwhelming might.

Sweet flowers seem gleaming 'mid the tangled grass
    Sparkling with spray-drops from the rushing rill,
And as these fleeting visions fade and pass
40   Perchance some pensive tears our eyes may fill.

These soon are wiped away, again we turn
    With fresh delight to the enchanted page

Where pictured thoughts that breathe and speak and burn
   Still please alike our youth and riper age.

45 There rises some lone rock all wet with surge
   And dashing billows glimmering in the light
Of a wan moon, whose silent rays emerge
   From clouds that veil their lustre, cold and bright.

And there 'mongst reeds upon a river's side
50   A wild bird sits, and brooding o'er her nest
Still guards the priceless gems, her joy and pride,
   Now ripening 'neath her hope-enlivened breast.

We turn the page: before the expectant eye
   A traveller stands lone on some desert heath;
55 The glorious sun is passing from the sky
   While fall his farewell rays on all beneath;

O'er the far hills a purple veil seems flung,
   Dim herald of the coming shades of night;
E'en now Diana's lamp aloft is hung,
60   Drinking full radiance from the fount of light.

Oh, when the solemn wind of midnight sighs,
   Where will the lonely traveller lay his head?
Beneath the tester of the star-bright skies
   On the wild moor he'll find a dreary bed.

65 Now we behold a marble Naiad placed
   Beside a fountain on her sculptured throne,
Her bending form with simplest beauty graced,
   Her white robes gathered in a snowy zone.

She from a polished vase pours forth a stream
70   Of sparkling water to the waves below
Which roll in light and music, while the gleam
   Of sunshine flings through shade a golden glow.

A hundred fairer scenes these leaves reveal;
   But there are tongues that injure while they praise:
75 I cannot speak the rapture that I feel
   When on the work of such a mind I gaze.

Then farewell, Bewick, genius' favoured son,
   Death's sleep is on the thee, all thy woes are past;
From earth departed, life and labour done,
80   Eternal peace and rest are thine at last.

4 *A National Ode for the Angrians*

The sun is on the Calabar, the dawn is quenched in day,
The stars of night are vanishing, her shadows flee away;

The sandy plains of Etrei flash back arising light,
And the wild wastes of Northangerland gleam bright as
      heaven is bright.

5   Zamorna lifts her fruitful hills like Eden's to the sky,
And fair as Enna's fields of flowers her golden prairies lie;

And Angria calls from mount and vale, from wood and
      heather-dell,
A song of joy and thankfulness on rushing winds to swell.

For Romalla has put his robe of regal purple on,
10   And from the crags of Pendlebrow the russet garb is gone;

And Boulsworth off his giant sides rolls down the vapours
      dim;
And Hawkscliffe's bright and bowery glades uplift their
      matin hymn.

The ancient hills of Sydenham have never felt the glow
Of such a dawn as that which burns their blushing
      summits now.

15   The fields and woods of Edwardston are full of song and
      dew;
Olympia's waves glance clear along their wandering line
      of blue.

Green Arundel has caught the ray upspringing from the
      East;
Guadima rolls exultingly with sunshine on its breast.

All Angria through her provinces to arms and glory cries:
20   Her sun is up and she has heard her battle-shout, 'Arise!'
My Kingdom's gallant gentlemen are gathered like a host:
With such a bold and noble band was never conflict lost!

For they would fight till the red blood burst in sweat-
       drops from their brow,
And never to the victor's yoke their lion-souls would bow.

25   Enara on the Douro's banks his serfs is gathering;
From hut and hall on the highland heath the sons of
       Warner spring;

And Howard o'er his breezy moors the bugle-blast has
       blown:
O Leopard! swift are the ready feet that answer to that
       tone.

The Gor-cock quailed at the summons shrill unconquered
       Agar sent;
30   A living whirlwind crossed the tracks that marked the
       withered bent;

Proud Moray called from the Calabar his vassals to the
       fight;
And the Lord of Southwood joyously has raised the flag
       of light.

Segovia's dark, Italian eye is lit with high-born pride;
The Chevalier of Arundel has bade his horsemen ride;

35   Young Stuart in the ranks of war uplifts his lofty plume;
And Roslyn like a red-deer bounds from the depths of
       mountain-gloom;

And Seymour's heir has heard a voice come from the
       ancient dead:
At once the ancestral dauntlessness through all his veins
       was shed.

But the sullen flag of Percy swells most proudly to the
       breeze

40 As haughtily the folds unfurl as if they swept the seas!
    Patrician Pirate! On each side his blighting glance is
          flung:
    The silent scorn that curls his lip can never know a
          tongue!

    Upon his melancholy brow a melancholy shade,
    Like snow-wreaths on Aornu's slope, eternally is laid.

45 But the son of that tremendous sire amid the throng
          appears, —
    His second self unpetrified by the chill lapse of years:

    A form of noblest energy, most sternly beautiful;
    A scymitar whose tempered edge no time can ever dull;

    A sword unflushed, a quenchless flame, a fixed and
          radiant star;
50 A noble steed caparisoned which snuffs the fight afar!

    The glory of his youthful brow, the light of his blue eye,
    Will flash upon the battle's verge like arrows of the sky.

    With such a host, with such a train, what hand can stop
          our path?
    Who can withstand the torrent's strength when it shall
          roll in wrath?

55 Lift, lift the scarlet banner up! Fling all its folds abroad,
    And let its blood-red lustre fall on Afric's blasted sod:

    For gore shall run where it has been, and blighted bones
          shall lie
    Wherever the sun standard swelled against the stormy
          sky.

    And when our battle-trumpets sound, and when our
          bugles sing.
60 The vulture from its distant rock shall spread its glancing
          wing;

And the gaunt wolf at that signal cry shall gallop to the
    feast:
A table in the wilderness we'll spread for bird and beast.

We'll sheath not the avenging sword till earth and sea and
    skies
Through all God's mighty universe shout back, 'Arise!
    Arise!'

65 Till Angria reigns Lord Paramount wherever human
    tongue
The 'Slaves' Lament,' the 'Emperor's Hymn,' in woe or
    bliss hath sung!

5 Retrospection

We wove a web in childhood,
    A web of sunny air;
We dug a spring in infancy
    Of water pure and fair;

5 We sowed in youth a mustard seed,
    We cut an almond rod;
We are now grown up to riper age:
    Are they withered in the sod?

Are they blighted, failed and faded,
10   Are they mouldered back to clay?
For life is darkly shaded,
    And its joys fleet fast away!

6 Stanzas

If thou be in a lonely place,
    If one hour's calm be thine,
As Evening bends her placid face
    O'er this sweet day's decline;

If all the earth and all the heaven
   Now look serene to thee,
As o'er them shuts the summer even,
   One moment – think of me!

Pause, in the lane, returning home;
   'Tis dusk, it will be still:
Pause near the elm, a sacred gloom
   Its breezeless boughs will fill.
Look at that soft and golden light,
   High in the unclouded sky;
Watch the last bird's belated flight,
   As it flits silent by.

Hark! for a sound upon the wind,
   A step, a voice, a sigh;
If all be still, then yield thy mind,
   Unchecked, to memory.
If thy love were like mine, how blest
   That twilight hour would seem,
When, back from the regretted Past,
   Returned our early dream!

If thy love were like mine, how wild
   Thy longings, even to pain,
For sunset soft, and moonlight mild,
   To bring that hour again?
But oft, when in thine arms I lay,
   I've seen thy dark eyes shine,
And deeply felt their changeful ray
   Spoke other love than mine.

My love is almost anguish now,
   It beats so strong and true;
'Twere rapture, could I deem that thou
   Such anguish ever knew.
I have been but thy transient flower,
   Thou wert my god divine,
Till checked by death's congealing power,
   This heart must throb for thine.

And well my dying hour were blest,
   If life's expiring breath
Should pass, as thy lips gently prest
   My forehead cold in death;
45   And sound my sleep would be, and sweet,
   Beneath the churchyard tree,
If sometimes in thy heart should beat
   One pulse, still true to me.

7 *The Teacher's Monologue*

The room is quiet, thoughts alone
   People its mute tranquillity;
The yoke put off, the long task done, –
   I am, as it is bliss to be,
5   Still and untroubled. Now, I see,
   For the first time, how soft the day
O'er waveless water, stirless tree,
   Silent and sunny, wings its way,
Now, as I watch the distant hill,
10   So faint, so blue, so far removed,
Sweet dreams of home my heart may fill,
   That home where I am known and loved:
It lies beyond; yon azure brow
   Parts me from all Earth holds for me;
15   And, morn and eve, my yearnings flow
   Thitherward tending, changelessly.
My happiest hours, ay! all the time,
   I love to keep in memory.
Lapsed among moors, ere life's first prime
20   Decayed to dark anxiety.

Sometimes, I think a narrow heart
   Makes me thus mourn those far away,
And keeps my love so far apart
   From friends and friendships of to-day;

25   Sometimes, I think 'tis but a dream
     I treasure up so jealously,
All the sweet thoughts I live on seem
     To vanish into vacancy:
And then, this strange, coarse world around
30   Seems all that's palpable and true;
And every sight and every sound
     Combine my spirit to subdue
To aching grief; so void and lone
     Is Life and Earth – so worse than vain,
35 The hopes that, in my own heart sown,
     And cherished by such sun and rain
As Joy and transient Sorrow shed,
     Have ripened to a harvest there:
Alas! methinks I hear it said,
40   'Thy golden sheaves are empty air.'
All fades away; my very home
     I think will soon be desolate;
I hear, at times, a warning come
     Of bitter partings at its gate;
45 And, if I should return and see
     The hearth-fire quenched, the vacant chair,
And hear it whispered mournfully,
     That farewells have been spoken there,
What shall I do, and whither turn?
50 Where look for peace? When cease to mourn?

'Tis not the air I wished to play,
     The strain I used to sing;
My wilful spirit slipped away
     And struck another string.
55 I neither wanted smile nor tear,
     Bright joy nor bitter woe,
But just a song that sweet and clear,
     Though haply sad, might flow.

A quiet song, to solace me
60   When sleep refused to come;

A strain to chase despondency
    When sorrowful for home.
In vain I try; I cannot sing;
    All feels so cold and dead;
65 No wild distress, no gushing spring
    Of tears in anguish shed;

But all the impatient gloom of one
    Who waits a distant day,
When, some great task of suffering done,
70   Repose shall toil repay.
For youth departs, and pleasure flies,
    And life consumes away,
And youth's rejoicing ardour dies
    Beneath this drear delay;

75 And Patience, weary with her yoke,
    Is yielding to despair,
And Health's elastic spring is broke
    Beneath the strain of care.
Life will be gone ere I have lived;
80   Where now is Life's first prime?
I've worked and studied, longed and grieved,
    Through all that rosy time.

To toil, to think, to long, to grieve, –
    Is such my future fate?
85 The morn was dreary, must the eve
    Be also desolate?
Well, such a life at least makes Death
    A welcome, wished-for friend;
Then, aid me, Reason, Patience, Faith,
90   To suffer to the end!

8 Parting

There's no use in weeping,
    Though we are condemned to part;

There's such a thing as keeping
    A remembrance in one's heart:

There's such a thing as dwelling
    On the thought ourselves have nursed,
And with scorn and courage telling
    The world to do its worst.

We'll not let its follies grieve us,
    We'll just take them as they come;
And then every day will leave us
    A merry laugh for home.

When we've left each friend and brother,
    When we're parted, wide and far,
We will think of one another,
    As even better than we are.

Every glorious sight above us,
    Every pleasant sight beneath,
We'll connect with those that love us,
    Whom we truly love till death!

In the evening, when we're sitting
    By the fire, perchance alone,
Then shall heart with warm heart meeting,
    Give responsive tone for tone.

We can burst the bonds which chain us,
    Which cold human hands have wrought,
And where none shall dare restrain us
    We can meet again, in thought.

So there's no use in weeping, –
    Bear a cheerful spirit still:
Never doubt that Fate is keeping
    Future good for present ill!

9 Life

Life, believe, is not a dream
　　So dark as sages say;
Oft a little morning rain
　　Foretells a pleasant day.
Sometimes there are clouds of gloom,
　　But these are transient all;
If the shower will make the roses bloom,
　　Oh, why lament its fall?
　　Rapidly, merrily,
Life's sunny hours flit by,
　　Gratefully, cheerily,
Enjoy them as they fly!

What though Death at times steps in,
　　And calls our best away?
What though Sorrow seems to win,
　　O'er Hope, a heavy sway?
Yet Hope again elastic springs,
　　Unconquered, though she fell;
Still buoyant are her golden wings,
　　Still strong to bear us well.
　　Manfully, fearlessly,
The day of trial bear,
　　For gloriously, victoriously,
Can courage quell despair!

10 A Valentine

A Roland for your Oliver
　　We think you've justly earned;
You sent us such a valentine,
　　Your gift is now returned.

We cannot write or talk like you;
　　We're plain folks every one;

You've played a clever jest on us,
  We thank you for the fun.

Believe us when we frankly say
  (Our words, though blunt, are true),
At home, abroad, by night or day,
  We all wish well to you.

And never may a cloud come o'er
  The sunshine of your mind;
Kind friends, warm hearts, and happy hours
  Through life, we trust, you'll find.

Where'er you go, however far
  In future years you stray,
There shall not want our earnest prayer
  To speed you on your way.

A stranger and a pilgrim here
  We know you sojourn now;
But brighter hopes, with brighter wreaths,
  Are doomed to bind your brow.

Not always in these lonely hills
  Your humble lot shall lie;
The oracle of fate foretells
  A worthier destiny.

And though her words are veiled in gloom,
  Though clouded her decree,
Yet doubt not that a juster doom
  She keeps in store for thee.

Then cast hope's anchor near the shore,
  'Twill hold your vessel fast,
And fear not for the tide's deep roar,
  And dread not for the blast.

For though this station now seems near,
  'Mid land-locked creeks to be,

The helmsman soon his ship will steer
    Out to the wide blue sea.

Well officered and staunchly manned,
    Well built to meet the blast;
With favouring winds the bark must land
    On glorious shores at last.

11 *Passion*

Some have won a wild delight,
    By daring wilder sorrow;
Could I gain thy love to-night,
    I'd hazard death to-morrow.

Could the battle-struggle earn
    One kind glance from thine eye,
How this withering heart would burn,
    The heady fight to try!

Welcome nights of broken sleep,
    And days of carnage cold,
Could I deem that thou wouldst weep
    To hear my perils told.

Tell me, if with wandering bands
    I roam full far away,
Wilt thou to those distant lands
    In spirit ever stray!

Wild, long, a trumpet sounds afar;
    Bid me – bid me go
Where Seik and Briton meet in war,
    On Indian Sutlej's flow.

Blood has dyed the Sutlej's waves
    With scarlet stain, I know;
Indus' borders yawn with graves,
    Yet, command me go!

25 Though rank and high the holocaust
   Of nations steams to heaven,
Glad I'd join the death-doomed host,
   Were but the mandate given.

Passion's strength should nerve my arm,
30   Its ardour stir my life,
Till human force to that dread charm
Should yield and sink in wild alarm,
   Like trees to tempest-strife.

If, hot from war, I seek thy love,
   Darest thou turn aside?
35 Darest thou then my fire reprove,
   By scorn, and maddening pride?

No – my will shall yet control
   Thy will so high and free,
And love shall tame that haughty soul –
40   Yes – tenderest love for me.

I'll read my triumph in thine eyes,
   Behold, and prove the change;
Then leave, perchance, my noble prize,
   Once more in arms to range.

45 I'd die when all the foam is up,
   The bright wine sparkling high;
Nor wait till in the exhausted cup
   Life's dull dregs only lie.

Then Love thus crowned with sweet reward,
50   Hope blessed with fulness large,
I'd mount the saddle, draw the sword,
   And perish in the charge!

12 *Evening Solace*

The human heart has hidden treasures,
    In secret kept, in silence sealed; –
The thoughts, the hopes, the dreams, the pleasures,
    Whose charms were broken if revealed.
5   And days may pass in gay confusion,
    And nights in rosy riot fly,
While, lost in Fame's or Wealth's illusion,
    The memory of the Past may die.

But there are hours of lonely musing,
10 Such as in evening silence come,
When, soft as birds their pinions closing,
    The heart's best feelings gather home.
Then in our souls there seems to languish
    A tender grief that is not woe;
15 And thoughts that once wrung groans of anguish,
    Now cause but some mild tears to flow.

And feelings, once as strong as passions,
    Float softly back – a faded dream;
Our own sharp griefs and wild sensations,
20   The tale of others' sufferings seem.
Oh! when the heart is freshly bleeding,
    How longs it for that time to be,
When, through the mist of years receding,
    Its woes live but in reverie!

25 And it can dwell on moonlight glimmer,
    On evening shade and loneliness;
And, while the sky grows dim and dimmer,
    Feel no untold and strange distress –
Only a deeper impulse given
30   By lonely hour and darkened room,
To solemn thoughts that soar to heaven
    Seeking a life and world to come.

13 'He saw my heart's woe'

He saw my heart's woe, discovered my soul's anguish,
   How in fever, in thirst, in atrophy it pined;
Knew he could heal, yet looked and let it languish,
   To its moans spirit-deaf, to its pangs spirit-blind.

5 But once a year he heard a whisper low and dreary
   Appealing for aid, entreating some reply;
Only when sick, soul-worn, and torture-weary,
   Breathed I that prayer, heaved I that sigh.

He was mute as is the grave, he stood stirless as a tower,
10 At last I looked up, and saw I prayed to stone:
I asked help of that which to help had no power,
   I sought love where love was utterly unknown.

Idolater I kneeled to an idol cut in rock!
   I might have slashed my flesh and drawn my heart's
     best blood:
15 The Granite God had felt no tenderness, no shock;
   My Baal had not seen nor heard nor understood.

In dark remorse I rose; I rose in darker shame;
   Self-condemned I withdrew to an exile from my kind;
A solitude I sought where mortal never came,
20 Hoping in its wilds forgetfulness to find.

Now, Heaven, heal the wound which I still deeply feel;
   Thy glorious hosts look not in scorn on our poor race;
Thy King eternal doth no iron judgement deal
   On suffering worms who seek forgiveness, comfort,
     grace.

25 He gave our hearts to love: He will not Love despise,
   E'en if the gift be lost, as mine was long ago;
He will forgive the fault, will bid the offender rise,
   Wash out with dews of bliss the fiery brand of woe;

And give a sheltered place beneath the unsullied throne,
30 Whence the soul redeemed may mark Time's fleeting
        course round earth;
And know its trials overpast, its sufferings gone,
    And feel the peril past of Death's immortal birth.

14 *On the Death of Emily Jane Brontë*

My darling, thou wilt never know
The grinding agony of woe
    That we have borne for thee.
Thus may we consolation tear
5 E'en from the depth of our despair
    And wasting misery.

The nightly anguish thou art spared
When all the crushing truth is bared
    To the awakening mind,
10 When the galled heart is pierced with grief,
Till wildly it implores relief,
    But small relief can find.

Nor know'st thou what it is to lie
Looking forth with streaming eye
15   On life's lone wilderness.
    'Weary, weary, dark and drear,
How shall I the journey bear,
    The burden and distress?'

Then since thou art spared such pain
20 We will not wish thee here again;
    He that lives must mourn.
God help us through our misery
And give us rest and joy with thee
    When we reach our bourne!

15 *On the Death of Anne Brontë*

There's little joy in life for me,
    And little terror in the grave;
I've lived the parting hour to see
    Of one I would have died to save.

5   Calmly to watch the failing breath,
    Wishing each sigh might be the last;
Longing to see the shade of death
    O'er those beloved features cast.

The cloud, the stillness that must part
10   The darling of my life from me;
And then to thank God from my heart,
    To thank Him well and fervently;

Although I knew that we had lost
    The hope and glory of our life;
15   And now, benighted, tempest-tossed,
    Must bear alone the weary strife.

POEMS BY PATRICK BRANWELL BRONTË

16 Augusta

Augusta! Though I'm far away
    Across the dark blue sea
Still eve and morn and night and day
    Will I remember Thee!

5
And though I cannot see thee nigh
    Or hear thee speak to me
Thy look and voice and memory
    Shall not forgotten be

I stand upon this Island shore
10
    A single hour alone
And see the Atlantic swell before
    With sullen surging tone

While high in heaven the full Moon glides
    Above the breezy deep
15
Unmoved by waves or winds or tides
    That far beneath her sweep

She marches through this midnight air
    So silent and divine
With not a wreath of vapour there
20
    To dim her silver shine

For every cloud through ether driven
    Has settled far below
And round the unmeasured skirts of heaven
    Their whitened fleeces glow

25   They join and part and pass away
       Beyond the heaving sea
   So mutable and restless they
       So still and changeless she

   Those clouds have melted into air
30   Those waves have sunk to sleep
   But clouds renewed are rising there
       And fresh waves crowd the deep

   How like the chaos of my soul
       Where visions ever rise
35   And thoughts and passions ceaseless roll
       And tumult never dies

   Each fancy but the former's grave
       And germ of that to come
   While all are fleeting as the wave
40   That chafes itself to foam

   I said that full Moon glides on high
       Howe'er the world repines
   And in its own untroubled sky
       For ever smiles and shines

45   So dark'ning o'er my anxious brow
       Though thicken cares and pain
   Within my Heart Augusta thou
       For ever shalt remain

   And Thou art not that wintry moon
50   With its melancholy ray
   But where thou shinest is summer noon
       And bright and perfect day

   The Moon sinks down as sinks the night
       But Thou beam'st brightly on
55   She only shines with borrowed light
       But Thine is all Thine Own!

17 *The Doubter's Hymn*

Life is a passing sleep
Its deeds a troubled dream
And death the dread awakening
To daylight's dawning beam

5   We sleep without a thought
Of what is past and o'er
Without a glimpse of consciousness
Of aught that lies before

We dream and on our sight
10   A thousand visions rise
Some dark as Hell some heavenly bright
But all are phantasies

We wake and oh how fast
These mortal visions fly!
15   Forgot amid the wonders vast
Of immortality!

And oh! when we arise
With 'wildered gaze to see
The aspect of those morning skies
20   Where will that waking be?

How will that Future seem?
What is Eternity?
Is Death the sleep? – Is Heaven the Dream?
Life the reality?

18 *Song*

Thou art gone but I am here
Left behind and mourning on
Doomed in Dreams to deem thee near
But to wake and find thee gone!

5   Ever parted! Broken hearted!
         Weary, wandering all alone!

       Looks and smiles that once were thine
         Rise before me night and day
       Telling me that thou *wert* mine
10   But *art* dead and passed away
       Beauty banished – Feelings vanished
         From thy dark and dull decay
       No returning! Naught but mourning
         O'er thy cold and coffined clay!

19 Memory

       Hours and days my Heart has lain
       Through a scene of changeless pain
       As it ne'er would wake again
         Sad and still and silently

5   Time has flown, but all unkown
       Nothing could arouse a tone
       Not a single string would moan
         In replying sympathy

       Memory Memory comes at last
10   Memory of feelings past
       And with an Eolian blast
         Strikes the strings resistlessly.

20 Mary's Prayer

       Remember me when Death's dark wing
         Has borne me far from thee;
       When, freed from all this suffering,
         My grave shall cover me.

5 Remember me, and, if I die
   To perish utterly,
Yet shrined within thy memory
   Thy Heart my Heaven shall be!

   'Twas all I wished, when first I gave
10   This hand unstained and free,
That I from thence might ever have
   A place, my lord, with thee.

So, if from off my dying bed
   Thou'dst banish misery,
15 Oh say that when I'm cold and dead
   Though wilt remember me!

21 *To Maecenas*

  Maecenas, sprung of kingly line,
My guardian and my guide divine;
Many there are whose pleasure lies
In striving for the victor's prize,
5 Whom dust clouds, drifting o'er the throng
As whirls the Olympic car along,
And kindling wheels, and close shunned goal
Amid the highest gods enrole.
One man perhaps his pleasure draws
10 From the inconstant crowd's applause;
Another seeks more solid gain
From granaries of Lybian grain;
The peaceful Farmer labours o'er
The Land his fathers ploughed before;
15 Nor these, from forum or from farm,
The wealth of Attalus could charm
To leave their homes, and seek a grave
Beneath the deep Aegean wave.
The Merchant, when 'at home at ease'
20 May shudder at tempestuous seas,

And, scarce escaped from ocean's roar,
May praise the pleasures of the shore;
Yet – shuddering too at poverty,
Again he seeks that very sea.
25   The son of pleasure, careless laid
Beside a fountain, neath the shade,
Will sometimes wish to wile away
With mellowed wine, a summer day;
Though others mother-hated war
30   With fife's and trumpet's mingled jar
To camps and combats calls afar.
The Hunter, neath a freezing sky,
Can banish from his memory
The tender wife he left at home,
35   O'er pathless wilds at will to roam;
If but his fleet hounds chase the deer;
Or Marsian boar his toils uptear.
But, Ivy garlands me adorn,
By them to heavenly honours born;
40   Yes, me swift nymphs and satyrs bear
To woods, apart from worldly care;
If but Euterpe yield to me
Her thrilling pipe of melody;
If Polyhymnia but inspire
45   My spirit with her Lesbian lyre.
Oh! give thy friend a poet's name,
And heaven shall hardly bound his fame!

22 To Thaliarchus

See'st thou not amid the skies,
White with snow, Soracte rise?
While the forests on the plain
Scarce their hoary weight sustain,
5   And congealed the waters stand
Neath the frost's arresting hand.

Drive away the winter wild;
On the hearth be fuel piled;
And, from its inmost cell
10   Kept in Sabine vase so well,
Generous, bring thy four years wine;
Brightest source of song divine!
   Wisely leave the rest to heaven,
Who, when warring winds have striven
15   With the forests or the main,
Bids their ragings rest again.
   Be not ever pondering
Over what the morn may bring;
Whether it be joy or pain
20   Wisely count it all as gain;
And, while age forbears to shed
Snows, or sorrows o'er thy head,
Do not scorn the dancers' feet,
Nor thy lovers dear retreat.
25   Hasten to the plain or square;
List the voice that whispers where,
While the calm night rules above,
Thou may'st meet thy constant love;
While the laugh round corner sly
30   May instruct thee where to spy;
While the wanton's feigned retreating
Still may leave some pledge of meeting;
Perhaps a ring or bracelet bright
Snatched from arm or finger white.

23 *'The desolate earth'*

The desolate earth, the wintry sky,
The ceaseless rain-showers driving by –
   The farewell of the year –
Though drear the sight, and sad the sound,

5   While bitter winds are wailing round,
       Nor hopes depress, nor thoughts confound,
          Nor waken sigh or tear.

       For, as it moans, December's wind
       Brings many varied thoughts to mind
10   Upon its storm-drenched wing,
       Of words, not said 'mid sunshine gay,
       Of deeds, not done in summer's day,
       Yet which, when joy has passed away,
          Will strength to sorrow bring.

15   For, when the leaves are glittering bright,
       And green hills lie in noonday night,
          The present only lives;
       But, when within my chimnies roar
       The chidings of the stormy shower,
20   The feeble present loses power,
          The mighty past survives.

       I cannot think – as roses blow,
       And streams sound gently in their flow,
          And clouds shine bright above –
25   Of aught but childhood's happiness,
       Of joys unshadowed by distress
       Or voices tuned the ear to bless
          Or faces made to love.

       But, when these winter evenings fall
30   Like dying nature's funeral pall,
          The Soul gains strength to say
       That – not aghast at stormy skies –
       That – not bowed down by miseries, –
       Its thoughts have will and power to rise
35   Above the present day.

       So, winds amid yon leafless ash,
       And yon swollen streamlet's angry dash,
          And yon wet howling sky,

Recall the victories of mind
40   O'er bitter heavens and stormy wind
And all the wars of humankind –
    Man's mightiest victory!

The darkness of a dungeon's gloom,
So oft ere death the spirit's tomb,
45   Could not becloud those eyes
Which first revealed to mortal sight
A thousand unknown worlds of light,
And that *one* grave shines best by night
    Where Galileo lies.

50   But – into drearier dungeons thrown,
With bodies bound, whose minds were gone –
    Tasso's immortal strain,
Despite the tyrant's stern decree,
Mezentius-like – rose fresh and free
55   And sang of Salem's liberty
    Forgetful of his chain;

And thou, great rival of his song,
Whose seraph-wings so swift and strong
    Left this world far behind,
60   Though poor, neglected, blind and old,
The clouds round Paradise unrolled
And in immortal accents told
    Misery must bow to mind.

See, in a garret bare and low,
65   While mighty London roars below,
    One poor man seated lone;
No favourite child of fortune he,
But owned as hers by Poverty,
His rugged brow, his stooping knee,
70   Speak woe and want alone.

Now, who would guess that yonder form,
Scarce worth being beaten by life's storm,
    Could e'er be known to fame?

Yet England's love and England's tongue,
75 And England's heart, shall reverence long
The wisdom deep, the courage strong,
    Of English *Johnson's* name.

Like him — foredoomed through life to bear
The anguish of the heart's despair
80   That pierces spirit through —
Sweet Cowper, 'mid his weary years,
Led through a rayless vale of tears,
Poured gentle wisdom on our ears,
    And his was English too.

85 But Scotland's desolate hills can show
How mind can triumph over woe,
    For many a cottage there,
Where ceaseless toil from day to day
Scarce keeps grim want one hour away,
90 Could show if known how great the sway
    Of spirit o'er despair.

And he whose natural music fills
Each wind that sweeps her heathy hills,
    Bore up with manliest brow
95 'Gainst griefs that ever filled his breast,
'Gainst toils that never gave him rest,
So, though grim fate Burns' life oppressed,
    His soul it could not bow.

24 *'The man who will not know another'*

'The man who will not know another,
    Whose heart can never sympathise,
Who loves not comrade, friend, or brother,
    Unhonoured lives — unnoticed dies.
5   His frozen eye, his bloodless heart,
Nature, repugnant, bids depart.

'O Grundy! born for nobler aim,
　　Be thine the task to shun such shame;
And henceforth never think that he
10　　　Who gives his hand in courtesy
To one who kindly feels to him,
His gentle birth or name can dim.

'However mean a man may be,
　　Know man *is* man as well as thee;
15　However high thy gentle line,
　　Know he who writes can rank with thine;
And though his frame be worn and dead,
Some light still glitters round his head.

'Yes! though his tottering limbs seem old,
20　　His heart and blood are not yet cold.
Ah, Grundy! shun his evil ways,
　　His restless nights, his troubled days;
But never slight his mind, which flies,
Instinct with noble sympathies,
25　Afar from spleen and treachery,
　　To thought, to kindness, and to thee.'

25 *Lord Nelson*

Man thinks too often that the ills of Life,
Its fruitless labours and its causeless strife,
Its fell disease, grim want and cankering care,
Must wage 'gainst Spirit a successful war;
5　That faint and feeble proves the struggling soul
'Mid the dark waves that ever round it roll;
That it can never triumph or feel free
While pain its body holds or poverty.
　　No words of mine have power to rouse the brain
10　Distressed with grief – the body bowed with pain;
They will not hear me if I prove how high
Man's soul can soar o'er body's misery.

But, where orations long and deep and loud
Are weak as air to move the listening crowd,
A single word, just then, if timely spoken,
The mass inert has roused, their silence broken,
And driven them shouting for revenge or fame,
Trampling on fear or death, led by a *single Name*.
So now to him whose worn out soul decays
'Neath nights of sleepless pain or toilsome days
Who thinks his feeble frame must vainly long
To tread the footsteps of the bold and strong,
Who thinks that, born beneath a lowly star,
He cannot climb those heights he sees from far,
To him I name one name (it needs but one)
NELSON, a world's defence, a kingdom's noblest son.

Ah! little child, torn early from thy home,
Over a desolate waste of waves to roam,
I see thy fair hair streaming in the wind
Wafted from green hills left so far behind –
A farewell given to thy English home,
And hot tears dimming all thy views of fame to come!

Then thou perhaps wert clinging to the mast,
Rocked high above the Northern Ocean's waste,
Stern accents only shouted from beneath,
Above, the keen wind's bitter biting breath,
And thy young eyes attentive to descry
The Ice-blink gleaming 'neath a Greenland sky;
All round, the presages of strife and storm
Engirdling thy young heart and feeble form;
Each change thy frame endured were fit to be
The total round of common destiny.
For next, upon the wild Mosquito shore
San Juan's guns their deadly thunders pour,
Though deadlier far that pestilential sky
Whose hot winds only whispered who should die.
Yet, while – forgotten – all their honours won –
Strong frames lay rotting 'neath a tropic sun

And mighty breasts heaved in death's agony,
50   Death only left the wind-worn *Nelson* free,
Left him to dare his darts through many a year
Of storm-tossed life – unbowed by pain or fear.

Death saw him laid on rocky Teneriffe,
Where sailors bore away their bleeding chief,
55   Struck down by shot and beaten back by fate,
Yet keeping Iron front and soul elate.

Death saw him, calm, off Copenhagen's shore,
Amid a thousand guns' death-dealing roar,
Triumphant riding o'er a fallen foe,
60   With hand prepared to strike, and heart to spare the
      blow.

Death touched, but left him, when a tide of blood
Stained the dark waves of Egypt's ancient flood,
When mighty L'Orient fired the midnight sky
And clouds dimmed Napoleon's destiny,
65   When 'neath that blaze flashed redly sea and shore,
When far Aboukir shook beneath its roar,
Then fell on all one mighty pause of dread
As if wide heaven were shattered overhead.
But from his pallet where the hero lay
70   His forehead laced with blood and pale as clay
He rose, revived by that tremendous call,
Forgot the blow which lately made him fall
And bade the affrighted battle hurry on,
Nor thought of pain or rest till victory was won.

75   I see him set – his coffin by his chair –
With pain-worn cheeks and wind-dishevelled hair,
A little shattered wreck from many a day
Of ocean storm and battle passed away,
Prepared at any hour God bade to die
80   But not to stop or rest or strike or fly;
While like a burning reed his spirit's flame

Brightened as it consumed its mortal frame.
He heard death tapping at his cabin door,
He knew his light'ning course must soon be o'er.

85   That he must meet the grim yet welcome guest,
Not on a palace bed of downy rest
But where the stormy waters rolled below,
And pealed, above, the thunders of the foe;
That no calm sleep must smooth a slow decay

90   Till scarce the watchers knew life passed away;
But stifling agony and gushing gore
Must tell the moments of his parting hour.
He knew, but smiled, for – as that Polar Star
For thousand years as then had shone from far

95   While all had changed beneath its changeless sky –
So what to earth belongs, on earth must die.
While he, all soul, should only take his flight
Like yon, through time, a soft and steady light;
Like yon, to England's sailors given to be

100 The guardian of their fleets, the pole star of the free.

A vessel lies in England's proudest port,
Where venerating thousands oft resort,
And though ships round her anchor, bold and gay,
They seek her only in her grim decay;

105 They tread her decks, all tenantless, with eyes
Of musing awe, not vulgar vain surprise;
They enter in a cabin, dark and low,
And o'er its time-stained floor in reverence bow.
There's nought to see but rafters worn and old.

110 No mirrored walls, no cornice bright with gold;
Yon packet, steaming through the smoky haze
Seems fitter far to suit the wanderers' gaze.
But – 'tis not present times they look on now,
They gaze on six and thirty years ago;

115 They see where fell the 'Thunder-bolt of war'
On the storm-swollen waves of *Trafalgar;*
They see the spot where fell a star of glory,
The Finis to one pace of England's story;

They read a tale to wake their pain and pride
120　In that brass plate engraved – 'HERE NELSON DIED.'

As 'wise Cornelius' from his mirror bade
A veil of formless cloudiness to fade,
Till gleamed before the awe-struck gazer's eye
Scenes still to come or passed for ever by,
125　So let me, standing in this darksome room,
Roll back its shapelessness of mourning gloom
And show the morn and evening of a Sun
The memory of whose light still cheers old England on.

Where ceaseless showers obscure the misty vale,
130　And winter winds through leafless osiers wail,
Beside yon swollen torrent rushing wild
Sits calm, amid the storm, that fair-haired child.
He *cannot* cross – so full the waters flow –
So bold his little heart – he *will not* go.
135　He has been absent, wandering many an hour,
As wild waves toss a solitary flower,
While from the old Rectory, his distant home,
'All hands' to seek their missing darling roam;
And *one* – his mother – with instinctive love,
140　Like that which guides aright the timid dove,
Finds her dear child, his cheeks all rain-bedewed,
The unconscious victim of those tempests rude,
And, panting, asks him why he tarries there –
Did he not dread his fate, his danger fear?
145　That child replies – all smiling 'mid the storm –
'Say Mother – what is this "fear"? I never saw his form.'

Oft since, he saw the waters howling round,
Oft heard unmoved, as then, the tempest sound,
Oft stood unshaken, death and danger near,
150　But knew no more than then the phantom *Fear*.

Now wave the wand again – let England's shore
Be lost amid a distant ocean's roar;
Return again this cabin, dark and grim,

Beheld through smoke-wreaths, indistinct and dim.
155 'Where is my child?' methinks the mother cries:
No – far away that mother's grave stone lies!
Where is her child? He is not surely here
Where reign 'mid storm and darkness Death and FEAR.

    A prostrate form lies 'neath a double shade
160 By stifling smoke and blackened rafters made,
With head that backward rolls whene'er it tries
From its hard thunder-shaken bed to rise.
Methought I saw a brightness on its breast,
As if in royal orders decked and dressed;
165 But that wan face, those grey locks crimson-dyed,
Have nought to do with human power or pride,
Where Death his mandate writes on that white brow:
'Thy earthly course is done – come with me now!'
Stern faces o'er this figure, weeping bend
170 As they had lost a father and a friend,
And all unnoticed burst yon conquering cheer
Since HE their glorious chief is dying here.
They heed it not; but, with rekindling eye,
As he even Death would conquer ere he die,
175 Asks: 'What was't? What deed had England done?
What ships had struck, was victory nobly won?
Did Collingwood – did Trowbridge face the foe?
Whose ship was first in fight, who dealt the sternest
     blow?'

I could not hear the answer, lost and drowned
180 In that tremendous crash of earthquake sound,
But I could see the dying hero smile,
For pain and sickness vanquished humbly bowed the
     while
TO SOUL, that soared prophetic o'er their sway,
And saw beyond Death's night Fame's glorious day,
185 That deemed no bed so easy as the tomb
In old Westminister's hero-sheltering gloom;
That knew the laurel round his dying brow

Must bloom for ever as it flourished now,
That felt this pain he paid was cheaply given
190 For endless fame on earth and joy in heaven.
It was a smile as sweet as ever shone
On that wan face in childhood long since gone,
A smile that asked as plainly:- 'What is fear?'
As then unnoticed though as then so near!
195 *That spirit cared not that his wornout form*
Was soon to be a comrade of the worm,
Nor shuddered at the icy hand of Death,
So soon – so painfully to stop his breath.

The guns were thundering fainter on his ear;
200 More, fading fast from sight that cabin drear;
The place, the hour became less clearly known:
He only felt that his great work was done,
That one brave heart was kneeling at his side,
So, murmuring 'Kiss me, Hardy,' Nelson, smiling, died.

205 But when *I* think upon that awful day
When all I know or love must fade away,
When, after weeks perhaps of agony,
Without a hope of aught to succour me,
I must lie back and close my eyes upon
210 The parting glories of God's holy sun
And feel his warmth I never more must know
Mocking my wretched frame of pain and woe,
Yes – feel his light is brightening up the sky
As shining clouds and summer airs pass by,
215 While I a shrouded corpse this bed must leave
To lie forgotten in my dreary grave,
The world all smiles above my covering clay,
I silent – senseless – festering fast away.

And if my children 'mongst the churchyard stones,
220 Years hence, should see a few brown mouldering bones,
Perhaps a skull that seems with hideous grin
To mock at all this world takes pleasure in,
They'd only from the unsightly relics turn,

Or into ranker grass the fragments spurn,
225 Nor know that those were the remains of him
Whom they remember like a happy dream;
Who kissed and danced them on a father's knee
In long departed hours of happy Infancy!

O Mighty Being! give me strength to dare
230 The certain fate – the dreadful hour to bear –
As thou didst, Nelson, 'mid that awful roar,
Lying pale with mortal sickness – choked with gore,
Yet thinking of thine ENGLAND, saved that hour
From her great Foeman's empire-crushing power;
235 Of thy poor frame, so gladly given to free
Her thousand happy homes from slavery;
Of stainless name for her – of endless fame for Thee!

Give me, Great God, give all beneath Thy sway,
Soul to command and body to obey;
240 When dangers threat – a heart to beat more high;
When doubts confuse – a more observant eye;
When fate would crush us down – a steadier arm;
A firmer front – as stronger beats the storm.
We are Thy likeness – give us on to go
245 Through life's long march of chance and change to woe,
Resolved Thine image shall be sanctified
By humble confidence, not foolish pride.
We have our task set – let us do it well;
Nor barter ease on earth with pain in hell.
250 We have our talents from Thy Treasury given:
Let us return Thee good account in Heaven.

I see Thy world – this age – is marching on,
Each year more wondrous than its parent gone;
And shall my own drag heavily and slow,
255 With wish to rise, yet grovelling far below?
Forbid it, God, who madst (me) what I am,
Nor made to honour let me bow to shame;
But as yon moon that *seems* through clouds to glide

Whose dark breasts ever strive her beams to hide
260 Shines *really* heedless of their earthly sway
In her own heaven of glory far away,

So may my soul, that seems involved below,
In life's conflicting mists of care and woe,
Far, far remote – from its own heaven – look down
265 On clouds of shining fleece or stormy frown,
And while – so oft eclipsed – men pity me,
Gaze steadfast at their life's inconstancy,
And feel myself, like her, at home in heaven with Thee.

26 *On Peaceful Death and Painful Life*

Why dost thou sorrow for the happy dead?
    For, if their life be lost, their toils are o'er,
    And woe and want can trouble them no more;
Nor ever slept they in an earthly bed
5 So sound as now they sleep, while dreamless laid
    In the dark chambers of the unknown shore,
    Where Night and Silence guard each sealed door.
So, turn from such as these thy drooping head,
    And mourn the *Dead Alive* – whose spirit flies –
10 Whose life departs, before his death has come;
    Who knows no Heaven beneath Life's gloomy skies,
Who sees no Hope to brighten up that gloom, –
    'Tis *He* who feels the worm that never dies, –
The *real* death and darkness of the tomb.

POEMS BY
EMILY JANE BRONTË

27 *'High waving heather'*

High waving heather, 'neath stormy blasts bending,
Midnight and moonlight and bright shining stars;
Darkness and glory rejoicingly blending,
Earth rising to heaven and heaven descending,
5   Man's spirit away from its drear dongeon sending,
Bursting the fetters and breaking the bars.

All down the mountain-sides, wild forests lending
One mighty voice to the life-giving wind;
Rivers their banks in the jubilee rending,
10   Fast through the valleys a reckless course wending,
Wilder and deeper their waters extending,
Leaving a desolate desert behind.

Shining and lowering and swelling and dying,
Changing for ever from midnight to noon;
15   Roaring like thunder, like soft music sighing,
Shadows on shadows advancing and flying,
Lightning-bright flashes the deep gloom defying,
Coming as swiftly and fading as soon.

28 *'Alone I sat'*

Alone I sat; the summer day
Had died in smiling light away;
I saw it die, I watched it fade
From misty hill and breezeless glade;

5   And thoughts in my soul were gushing,
And my heart bowed beneath their power;
And tears within my eyes were rushing
Because I could not speak the feeling,
The solemn joy around me stealing
10 In that divine, untroubled hour.

I asked myself: 'O why has heaven
Denied the precious gift to me,
The glorious gift to many given
To speak their thoughts in poetry?

15 'Dreams have encircled me,' I said,
'From careless childhood's sunny time;
Visions by ardent fancy fed
Since life was in its morning prime.'

But now, when I had hoped to sing,
20 My fingers strike a tuneless string;
And still the burden of the strain
Is: 'Strive no more; 'tis all in vain.'

29 'The old church tower'

The old church tower and garden wall
Are black with autumn rain,
And dreary winds foreboding call
The darkness down again.

5   I watched how evening took the place
Of glad and glorious day;
I watched a deeper gloom efface
The evening's lingering ray.

And as I gazed on the cheerless sky
10 Sad thoughts rose in my mind . . .

30 'The night is darkening round me'

The night is darkening round me,
The wild winds coldly blow;
But a tyrant spell has bound me
And I cannot, cannot go.

5   The giant trees are bending
Their bare boughs weighed with snow,
The storm is fast descending
And yet I cannot go.

Clouds beyond clouds above me,
10   Wastes beyond wastes below;
But nothing drear can move me;
I will not, cannot go.

31 'I'll come when thou art saddest'

I'll come when thou art saddest,
Laid alone in the darkened room;
When the mad day's mirth has vanished,
And the smile of joy is banished
5   From evening's chilly gloom.

I'll come when the heart's real feeling
Has entire, unbiassed sway,
And my influence o'er thee stealing,
Grief deepening, joy congealing,
10   Shall bear thy soul away.

Listen, 'tis just the hour,
The awful time for thee;
Dost thou not feel upon thy soul
A flood of strange sensations roll,
15   Forerunners of a sterner power,
Heralds of me?

32 'There are two trees'

There are two trees in a lonely field;
They breathe a spell to me;
A dreary thought their dark boughs yield,
All waving solemnly.

33 Last Words

I knew not 'twas so dire a crime
To say the word, Adieu;
But this shall be the only time
My slighted heart shall sue.

5   The wild moorside, the winter morn,
The gnarled and ancient tree –
If in your breast they waken scorn,
Shall wake the same in me.

I can forget black eyes and brows,
10   And lips of rosy charm,
If you forget the sacred vows
Those faithless lips could form.

If hard commands can tame your love,
Or prison walls can hold,
15   I would not wish to grieve above
A thing so false and cold.

And there are bosoms bound to mine
With links both tried and strong;
And there are eyes whose lightning shine
20   Has warmed and blest me long:

Those eyes shall make my only day,
Shall set my spirit free,
And chase the foolish thoughts away
That mourn your memory.

34 'Light up thy halls'

Light up thy halls! 'Tis closing day;
I'm drear and lone and far away —
Cold blows on my breast the northwind's bitter sigh,
And oh, my couch is bleak beneath the rainy sky!

5   Light up thy halls — and think not of me;
That face is absent now, thou hast hated so to see —
Bright be thine eyes, undimmed their dazzling shine,
For never, never more shall they encounter mine!

The desert moor is dark; there is tempest in the air;
10 I have breathed my only wish in one last, one burning
      prayer —
A prayer that would come forth, although it lingered
      long;
That set on fire my heart, but froze upon my tongue.

And now, it shall be done before the morning rise:
I will not watch the sun ascend in yonder skies.
15 One task alone remains — thy pictured face to view;
And then I go to prove if God, at least, be true!

Do I not see thee now? Thy black resplendent hair;
Thy glory-beaming brow, and smile, how heavenly fair!
Thine eyes are turned away — those eyes I would not see;
20 Their dark, their deadly ray, would more than madden
      me.
There, go, Deceiver, go! My hand is streaming wet;
My heart's blood flows to buy the blessing — To forget!
Oh could that lost heart give back, back again to thine,
One tenth part of the pain that clouds my dark decline!

25 Oh could I see thy lids weighed down in cheerless woe;
Too full to hide their tears, too stern to overflow;
Oh could I know thy soul with equal grief was torn,
This fate might be endured — this anguish might be borne!

How gloomy grows the night! 'Tis Gondal's wind that
        blows;
30 I shall not tread again the deep glens where it rose –
I feel it on my face – 'Where, wild blast, dost thou roam?
What do we, wanderer, here, so far away from home?

'I do not need thy breath to cool my death-cold brow;
But go to that far land, where she is shining now;
35 Tell Her my latest wish, tell Her my dreary doom;
Say that *my* pangs are past, but *Hers* are yet to come.'

Vain words – vain frenzied thoughts! No ear can hear my
        call –
Lost in the vacant air my frantic curses fall –
And could she see me now, perchance her lip would smile,
40 Would smile in careless pride and utter scorn the while!

But yet for all her hate, each parting glance would tell
A stronger passion breathed, burned, in this last farewell
Unconquered in my soul the Tyrant rules me still;
Life bows to my control, but *Love* I cannot kill!

35 *Stanzas*

Loud without the wind was roaring
    Through the waned autumnal sky;
Drenching wet, the cold rain pouring
    Spoke of stormy winters nigh.

5   All too like that dreary eve
    Sighed within repining grief;
Sighed at first, but sighed not long –
Sweet – How softly sweet it came!
Wild words of an ancient song,
10   Undefined, without a name.

'It was spring, for the skylark was singing.'
    Those words, they awakened a spell –

They unlocked a deep fountain whose springing
Nor Absence nor Distance can quell.

15   In the gloom of a cloudy November,
They uttered the music of May;
They kindled the perishing ember
Into fervour that could not decay.

Awaken on all my dear moorlands
20   The wind in its glory and pride!
O call me from valleys and highlands
To walk by the hill-river's side!

It is swelled with the first snowy weather;
The rocks they are icy and hoar,
25   And darker waves round the long heather,
And the fern-leaves are sunny no more.

There are no yellow-stars on the mountain,
The blue-bells have long died away
From the brink of the moss-bedded fountain,
30   From the side of the wintery brae –

But lovelier than cornfields all waving
In emerald and scarlet and gold
Are the slopes where the north-wind is raving,
And the glens where I wandered of old.

35   'It was morning, the bright sun was beaming.'
How sweetly that brought back to me
The time when nor labour nor dreaming
Broke the sleep of the happy and free.

But blithely we rose as the dusk heaven
40   Was melting to amber and blue;
And swift were the wings to our feet given
While we traversed the meadows of dew,

For the moors, for the moors where the short grass
Like velvet beneath us should lie!

45 For the moors, for the moors where each high pass
Rose sunny against the clear sky!

For the moors where the linnet was trilling
Its song on the old granite stone;
Where the lark – the wild sky-lark was filling
50 Every breast with delight like its own.

What language can utter the feeling
That rose when, in exile afar,
On the brow of a lonely hill kneeling
I saw the brown heath growing there.

55 It was scattered and stunted, and told me
That soon even that would be gone;
It whispered, 'The grim walls enfold me;
I have bloomed in my last summer's sun.'

But not the loved music whose waking
60 Makes the soul of the Swiss die away
Has a spell more adored and heart-breaking
Than in its half-blighted bells lay.

The spirit that bent 'neath its power,
How it longed, how it burned to be free!
65 If I could have wept in that hour
Those tears had been heaven to me.

Well, well, the sad minutes are moving
Though loaded with trouble and pain;
And sometimes the loved and the loving
70 Shall meet on the mountains again.

36 Stanzas

A little while, a little while,
The noisy crowd are barred away;
And I can sing and I can smile
A little while I've holyday!

5   Where wilt thou go, my harassed heart?
     Full many a land invites thee now;
     And places near and far apart
     Have rest for thee, my weary brow.

     There is a spot mid barren hills
10   Where winter howls and driving rain,
     But if the dreary tempest chills
     There is a light that warms again.

     The house is old, the trees are bare
     And moonless bends the misty dome
15   But what on earth is half so dear,
     So longed for as the hearth of home?

     The mute bird sitting on the stone,
     The dank moss dripping from the wall,
     The garden-walk with weeds o'er-grown,
20   I love them – how I love them all!

     Shall I go there? or shall I seek
     Another clime, another sky,
     Where tongues familiar music speak
     In accents dear to memory?

25   Yes, as I mused, the naked room,
     The flickering firelight died away
     And from the midst of cheerless gloom
     I passed to bright, unclouded day –

     A little and a lone green lane,
30   That opened on a common wide;
     A distant, dreamy, dim blue chain
     Of mountains circling every side;

     A heaven so clear, an earth so calm,
     So sweet, so soft, so hushed an air
35   And, deepening still the dream-like charm,
     Wild moor-sheep feeding everywhere –

That was the scene; I knew it well,
I knew the path-ways far and near
That winding o'er each billowy swell
40 Marked out the tracks of wandering deer.

Could I have lingered but an hour
It well had paid a week of toil,
But truth has banished fancy's power;
I hear my dungeon bars recoil –

45 Even as I stood with raptured eye
Absorbed in bliss so deep and dear
My hour of rest had fleeted by
And given me back to weary care.

37 *The Bluebell*

The blue bell is the sweetest flower
That waves in summer air;
Its blossoms have the mightiest power
To soothe my spirit's care.

5 There is a spell in purple heath
Too wildly, sadly dear;
The violet has a fragrant breath,
But fragrance will not cheer.

The trees are bare, the sun is cold,
10 And seldom, seldom seen;
The heavens have lost their zone of gold
The earth its robe of green;

And ice upon the glancing stream
Has cast its sombre shade
15 And distant hills and valleys seem
In frozen mist arrayed.

The blue bell cannot charm me now,
The heath has lost its bloom,

The violets in the glen below
20   They yield no sweet perfume.

But though I mourn the heather-bell
'Tis better far, away;
I know how fast my tears would swell
To see it smile to-day;

25   And that wood flower that hides so shy
Beneath its mossy stone
Its balmy scent and dewy eye:
'Tis not for them I moan.

It is the slight and stately stem,
30   The blossoms silvery blue,
The buds hid like a sapphire gem
In sheaths of emerald hue.

'Tis these that breathe upon my heart
A calm and softening spell
35   That if it makes the tear-drop start
Has power to soothe as well.

For these I weep, so long divided
Through winter's dreary day,
In longing weep – but most when guided
40   On withered banks to stray.

If chilly then the light should fall
Adown the dreary sky
And gild the dank and darkened wall
With transient brilliancy,

45   How do I yearn, how do I pine
For the time of flowers to come,
And turn me from that fading shine
To mourn the fields of home.

38 'I am the only being whose doom'

I am the only being whose doom
No tongue would ask, no eye would mourn;
I never caused a thought of gloom,
A smile of joy, since I was born.

5   In secret pleasure, secret tears,
This changeful life has slipped away,
As friendless after eighteen years,
As lone as on my natal day.

There have been times I cannot hide,
10   There have been times when this was drear,
When my sad soul forgot its pride
And longed for one to love me here.

But those were in the early glow
Of feelings since subdued by care;
15   And they have died so long ago,
I hardly now believe they were.

First melted off the hope of youth
Then fancy's rainbow fast withdrew;
And then experience told me truth
20   In mortal bosoms never grew.

'Twas grief enough to think mankind
All hollow, servile, insincere;
But worse to trust to my own mind
And find the same corruption there.

39 'And now the house-dog stretched once more'

And now the house-dog stretched once more
His limbs upon the glowing floor;
The children half resumed their play,
Though from the warm hearth scared away.
5   The goodwife left her spinning-wheel,

And spread with smiles the evening meal;
The shepherd placed a seat and pressed
To their poor fare his unknown guest.
And he unclasped his mantle now,
And raised the covering from his brow;
Said, 'Voyagers by land and sea
Were seldom feasted daintily';
And checked his host by adding stern
He'd no refinement to unlearn.
A silence settled on the room;
The cheerful welcome sank to gloom;
But not those words, though cold and high,
So froze their hospitable joy.
No – there was something in his face,
Some nameless thing they could not trace,
And something in his voice's tone
Which turned their blood as chill as stone.
The ringlets of his long black hair
Fell o'er a cheek most ghastly fair.
Youthful he seemed – but worn as they
Who spend too soon their youthful day.
When his glance drooped, 'twas hard to quell
Unbidden feelings' sudden swell;
And pity scarce her tears could hide,
So sweet that brow, with all its pride;
But when upraised his eye would dart
An icy shudder through the heart.
Compassion changed to horror then
And fear to meet that gaze again.
It was not hatred's tiger-glare,
Nor the wild anguish of despair;
It was not useless misery
Which mocks at friendship's sympathy.
No – lightning all unearthly shone
Deep in that dark eye's circling zone,
Such withering lightning as we deem

None but a spectre's look may beam;
And glad they were when he turned away
And wrapt him in his mantle grey,
45   Leant down his head upon his arm
And veiled from view their basilisk charm.

40 *'There was a time when my cheek burned'*

There was a time when my cheek burned
To give such scornful fiends the lie;
Ungoverned nature madly spurned
The law that bade it not defy.
5   O in the days of ardent youth
I would have given my life for truth.

For truth, for right, for liberty,
I would have gladly, freely died;
And now I calmly hear and see
10   The vain man smile, the fool deride;
Though not because my heart is tame,
Though not for fear, though not for shame.

My soul still chafes at every tone
Of selfish and self-blinded error;
15   My breast still braves the world alone,
Steeled as it ever was to terror;
Only I know, howe'er I frown,
The same world will go rolling on.

41 *Love and Friendship*

Love is like the wild rose-briar,
Friendship like the holly-tree –
The holly is dark when the rose-briar blooms
But which will bloom most constantly?

5   The wild rose-briar is sweet in spring,
       Its summer blossoms scent the air;
       Yet wait till winter comes again,
       And who will call the wild-briar fair?

       Then, scorn the silly rose-wreath now
10   And deck thee with the holly's sheen,
       That when December blights thy brow
       He still may leave thy garland green.

42 *Stanzas to* __

       'Well, some may hate, and some may scorn,
       And some may quite forget thy name,
       But my sad heart must ever mourn
       Thy ruined hopes, thy blighted fame.'

5   'Twas thus I thought, an hour ago,
       Even weeping o'er that wretch's woe.
       One word turned back my gushing tears.
       And lit my altered eye with sneers.

       'Then bless the friendly dust,' I said,
10   'That hides thy unlamented head.
       Vain as thou wert, and weak as vain,
       The slave of falsehood, pride, and pain,
       My heart has nought akin to thine –
       Thy soul is powerless over mine.'

15   But these were thoughts that vanished too –
       Unwise, unholy, and untrue –
       Do I despise the timid deer
       Because his limbs are fleet with fear?
       Or would I mock the wolf's death-howl
20   Because his form is gaunt and foul?
       Or hear with joy the leveret's cry
       Because it cannot bravely die?

No! Then above his memory
Let pity's heart as tender be:
25   Say, 'Earth lie lightly on that breast,
And, kind Heaven, grant that spirit rest!'

43 *'That wind I used to hear it swelling'*

That wind, I used to hear it swelling
With joy divinely deep;
You might have seen my hot tears welling,
But rapture made me weep.

5   I used to love on winter nights
To lie and dream alone
Of all the rare and real delights
My early years had known;

And oh, above the rest of those
10   That coming time should bear,
Like heaven's own glorious stars they rose
Still beaming bright and fair.

44 *Sympathy*

There should be no despair for you
While nightly stars are burning,
While evening pours its silent dew
And sunshine gilds the morning.

5   There should be no despair, though tears
May flow down like a river:
Are not the best beloved of years
Around your heart forever?

They weep – you weep – it must be so;
10   Winds sigh as you are sighing;
And Winter sheds its grief in snow
Where Autumn's leaves are lying:

Yet these revive, and from their fate
Your fate cannot be parted,
Then journey on, if not elate,
Still, *never* broken-hearted!

45 *Stanzas*

I'll not weep that thou art going to leave me,
There's nothing lovely here;
And doubly will the dark world grieve me
While thy heart suffers there.

I'll not weep, because the summer's glory
Must always end in gloom;
And, follow out the happiest story –
It closes with a tomb!

And I am weary of the anguish
Increasing winters bear;
Weary to watch the spirit languish
Through years of dead despair.

So, if a tear, when thou art dying,
Should haply fall from me,
It is but that my soul is sighing
To go and rest with thee.

46 *The Appeal*

If grief for grief can touch thee,
If answering woe for woe,
If any ruth can melt thee,
Come to me now!

I cannot be more lonely,
More drear I cannot be!
My worn heart throbs so wildly,
'Twill break for thee.

And when the world despises,
When heaven repels my prayer,
Will not mine angel comfort?
Mine idol hear?

Yes, by the tears I've poured thee,
By all my hours of pain,
O I shall surely win thee,
Beloved, again!

47 *The Night Wind*

In summer's mellow midnight,
A cloudless moon shone through
Our open parlour window
And rosetrees wet with dew.

I sat in silent musing,
The soft wind waved my hair:
It told me Heaven was glorious,
And sleeping Earth was fair.

I needed not its breathing
To bring such thoughts to me;
But still it whispered lowly;
'How dark the woods will be!

'The thick leaves in my murmur
Are rustling like a dream,
And all their myriad voices
Instinct with spirit seem.'

I said, 'Go, gentle singer,
Thy wooing voice is kind,
But do not think its music
Has power to reach my mind.

'Play with the scented flower,
The young tree's supple bough,
And leave my human feelings
In their own course to flow.'

25   The wanderer would not leave me;
Its kiss grew warmer still –
'O come,' it sighed so sweetly,
'I'll win thee 'gainst thy will.

'Have we not been from childhood friends?
30   Have I not loved thee long?
As long as thou hast loved the night
Whose silence wakes my song.

'And when thy heart is laid at rest
Beneath the church-yard stone
35   I shall have time enough to mourn
And thou to be alone.'

48 *The Caged Bird*

And like myself lone, wholly lone,
It sees the day's long sunshine glow;
And like myself it makes its moan
In unexhausted woe.

5   Give we the hills our equal prayer:
Earth's breezy hills and heaven's blue sea;
We ask for nothing further here
But our own hearts and liberty.

Ah! could my hand unlock its chain,
10   How gladly would I watch it soar,
And ne'er regret and ne'er complain
To see its shining eyes no more.

But let me think that if to-day
It pines in cold captivity,

15   To-morrow both shall soar away
            Eternally, entirely Free.

49 'Methinks this heart should rest awhile'

        Methinks this heart should rest awhile,
        So stilly round the evening falls;
        The veiled sun sheds no parting smile,
        Nor mirth, nor music wakes my halls.

5   I have sat lonely all the day,
        Watching the drizzly mist descend
        And first conceal the hills in grey
        And then along the valleys wend.

        And I have sat and watched the trees
10   And the sad flowers – how drear they blow:
        Those flowers were formed to feel the breeze
        Wave their light leaves in summer's glow.

        Yet their lives passed in gloomy woe
        And hopeless comes its dark decline,
15   And I lament, because I know
        That cold departure pictures mine.

50 The Old Stoic

        Riches I hold in light esteem
        And Love I laugh to scorn
        And lust of Fame was but a dream,
        That vanished with the morn –

5   And if I pray, the only prayer
        That moves my lips for me
        Is – 'Leave the heart that now I bear
        And give me liberty.'

Yes, as my swift days near their goal
'Tis all that I implore –
In life and death a chainless soul,
With courage to endure!

51 'Shall Earth no more inspire thee'

Shall Earth no more inspire thee,
Thou lonely dreamer now?
Since passion may not fire thee
Shall Nature cease to bow?

Thy mind is ever moving
In regions dark to thee;
Recall its useless roving –
Come back, and dwell with me.

I know my mountain breezes
Enchant and soothe thee still –
I know my sunshine pleases
Despite thy wayward will.

When day with evening blending
Sinks from the summer sky,
I've seen thy spirit bending
In fond idolatry.

I've watched thee every hour;
I know my mighty sway:
I know my magic power
To drive thy griefs away.

Few hearts to mortals given
On earth so wildly pine;
Yet few would ask a Heaven
More like this Earth than thine.

Then let my winds caress thee;
Thy comrade let me be –

Since nought beside can bless thee,
Return and dwell with me.

52 'I see around me tombstones grey'

I see around me tombstones grey
Stretching their shadows far away.
Beneath the turf my footsteps tread
Lie low and lone the silent dead;
Beneath the turf, beneath the mould —
Forever dark, forever cold,
And my eyes cannot hold the tears
That memory hoards from vanished years;
For Time and Death and Mortal pain
Give wounds that will not heal again.
Let me remember half the woe
I've seen and heard and felt below,
And Heaven itself, so pure and blest,
Could never give my spirit rest.
Sweet land of light! thy children fair
Know nought akin to our despair;
Nor have they felt, nor can they tell
What tenants haunt each mortal cell,
What gloomy guests we hold within —
Torments and madness, tears and sin!
Well, may they live in ecstasy
Their long eternity of joy;
At least we would not bring them down
With us to weep, with us to groan.
No — Earth would wish no other sphere
To taste her cup of sufferings drear;
She turns from Heaven a careless eye,
And only mourns that *we* must die!
Ah, mother, what shall comfort thee
In all this boundless misery?
To cheer our eager eyes a while

We see thee smile; how fondly smile!
But who reads not through that tender glow
Thy deep, unutterable woe?
35   Indeed, no dazzling land above
Can cheat thee of thy children's love.
We all, in life's departing shine,
Our last dear longings blend with thine,
And struggle still and strive to trace
40   With clouded gaze, thy darling face.
We would not leave our native home
For *any* world beyond the Tomb.
No – rather on thy kindly breast
Let us be laid in lasting rest;
45   Or waken but to sare with thee
A mutual immortality.

53   *How Clear She Shines!*

How clear she shines! how quietly
I lie beneath her guardian light
While Heaven and Earth are whispering me,
'To-morrow, wake, but dream to-night.'

5   Yes, Fancy, come, my Fairy love!
These throbbing temples, softly kiss;
And bend my lonely couch above
And bring me rest and bring me bliss.

The world is going – Dark world, adieu!
10   Grim world, conceal thee till the day;
The heart thou canst not all subdue
Must still resist if thou delay!

Thy love I will not, will not share;
Thy hatred only wakes a smile;
15   Thy griefs may wound – thy wrongs may tear,
But, oh, thy lies shall ne'er beguile!

While gazing on the stars that glow
Above me in that stormless sea,
I long to hope that all the woe
20   Creation knows, is held in thee!

And this shall be my dream to-night –
I'll think the heaven of glorious spheres
Is rolling on its course of light
In endless bliss through endless years;

25   I'll think there's not one world above,
Far as these straining eyes can see,
Where Wisdom ever laughed at Love,
Or Virtue crouched to Infamy;

Where, writhing 'neath the strokes of Fate,
30   The mangled wretch was forced to smile;
To match his patience 'gainst her hate,
His heart rebellious all the while;

Where Pleasure still will lead to wrong,
And helpless Reason warn in vain;
35   And Truth is weak and Treachery strong;
And Joy the surest path to Pain;

And Peace, the lethargy of Grief;
And Hope, a phantom of the soul;
And Life, a labour void and brief;
40   And Death, the despot of the whole!

54 'Yes, holy be thy resting place'

Yes, holy be thy resting place
Wherever thou may'st lie;
The sweetest winds breathe on thy face,
The softest of the sky.

5   And will not guardian Angles send
     Kind dreams and thoughts of love,
     Though I no more may watchful bend
     Thy longed repose above?

     And will not heaven itself bestow
10   A beam of glory there
     That summer's grass more green may grow,
     And summer's flowers more fair?

     Farewell, farewell, 'tis hard to part
     Yet, loved one, it must be:
15   I would not rend another heart
     Not even by blessing thee.

     Go! We must break affection's chain,
     Forget the hopes of years:
     Nay, grieve not – willest thou remain
20   To waken wilder tears?

     This wild breeze with thee and me,
     Roved in the dawning day:
     And thou shouldest be where it shall be
     Ere evening, far away.

55 *Warning and Reply*

     In the earth, the earth, thou shalt be laid,
     A grey stone standing over thee;
     Black mould beneath thee spread
     And black mould to cover thee.

5   'Well, there is rest there,
     So fast come thy prophecy;
     The time when my sunny hair
     Shall with grass roots twinèd be.'

     But cold, cold is that resting place,
10   Shut out from Joy and Liberty,

And all who loved thy living face
Will shrink from its gloom and thee.

'Not so: *here* the world is chill,
And sworn friends fall from me;
But *there*, they'll own me still
And prize my memory.'

Farewell, then, all that love,
All that deep sympathy:
Sleep on; heaven laughs above,
Earth never misses thee.

Turf-sod and tombstone drear
Part human company;
One heart broke only there –
That heart was worthy thee!

56 *Castle Wood*

The day is done, the winter sun
Is setting in its sullen sky;
And drear the course that has been run,
And dim the beams that slowly die.

No star will light my coming night;
No moon of hope for me will shine;
I mourn not heaven would blast my sight,
And I never longed for ways divine.

Through Life hard Task I did not ask
Celestial aid, celestial cheer;
I saw my fate without its mask,
And met it too without a tear.

The grief that prest this living breast
Was heavier far than earth can be;
And who would dread eternal rest
When labour's hire was agony?

Dark falls the fear of this despair
On spirits born for happiness;
But I was bred the mate of care,
The foster-child of sore distress.

No sighs for me, no sympathy,
No wish to keep my soul below;
The heart is dead since infancy,
Unwept for let the body go.

57 'Fall, leaves, fall'

Fall, leaves, fall; die, flowers, away;
Lengthen night and shorten day;
Every leaf speaks bliss to me
Fluttering from the autumn tree.
I shall smile when wreaths of snow
Blossom where the rose should grow;
I shall sing when night's decay
Ushers in a drearier day.

58 'All day I've toiled'

All day I've toiled, but not with pain,
In learning's golden mine;
And now at eventide again
The moonbeams softly shine.

There is no snow upon the ground,
No frost on wind or wave;
The south wind blew with gentlest sound,
And broke their icy grave.

'Tis sweet to wander here at night,
To watch the winter die,
With heart as summer sunshine light,
And warm as summer sky.

O may I never lose the peace
That lulls me gently now,
Though time should change my youthful face,
And years should shade my brow!

True to myself, and true to all,
May I be healthful still,
And turn away from passion's call,
And curb my own wild will.

59 *The Wanderer from the Fold*

How few, of all the hearts that loved,
Are grieving for thee now!
And why should mine, to-night, be moved
With such a sense of woe?

Too often, thus, when left alone
Where none my thoughts can see,
Comes back a word, a passing tone
From thy strange history.

Sometimes I seem to see thee rise,
A glorious child again –
All virtues beaming from thine eyes
That ever honoured men –

Courage and Truth, a generous breast
Where Love and Gladness lay;
A being whose very Memory blest
And made the mourner gay.

O fairly spread thy early sail,
And fresh and pure and free
Was the first impulse of the gale
That urged life's wave for thee!

Why did the pilot, too confiding,
Dream o'er that Ocean's foam,

And trust in Pleasure's careless guiding
To bring his vessel home?

25   For well he knew what dangers frowned,
What mists would gather dim;
What rocks and shelves and sands lay round
Between his port and him.

The very brightness of the sun,
30   The splendour of the main,
The wind that bore him wildly on
Should not have warned in vain.

An anxious gazer from the shore,
I marked the whitening wave,
35   And wept above thy fate the more
Because I could not save.

It recks not now, when all is over;
But yet my heart will be
A mourner still, though friend and lover
40   Have both forgotten thee!

60 Song

The linnet in the rocky dells,
The moor-lark in the air,
The bee among the heather-bells
That hide my lady fair:

5   The wild deer browse above her breast;
The wild birds raise their brood;
And they, her smiles of love caressed,
Have left her solitude!

I ween, that when the grave's dark wall
10   Did first her form retain,
They thought their hearts could ne'er recall
The light of joy again.

They thought the tide of grief would flow
Unchecked through future years,
15 But where is all their anguish now,
And where are all their tears?

Well, let them fight for Honour's breath,
Or Pleasure's shade pursue –
The Dweller in the land of Death
20 Is changed and careless too.

And if their eyes should watch and weep
Till sorrow's source were dry,
She would not, in her tranquil sleep,
Return a single sigh.

25 Blow, west wind, by the lonely mound,
And murmur, summer streams,
There is no need of other sound
To soothe my Lady's dreams.

61 *To Imagination*

When weary with the long day's care,
And earthly change from pain to pain,
And lost, and ready to despair,
Thy kind voice calls me back again –
5 O my true friend, I am not lone
While thou canst speak with such a tone!

So hopeless is the world without,
The world within I doubly prize;
Thy world where guile and hate and doubt
10 And cold suspicion never rise;
Where thou and I and Liberty
Have undisputed sovereignty.

What matters is that all around
Danger, and guilt, and darkness lie,
15 If but within our bosom's bound

We hold a bright, untroubled sky,
Warm with ten thousand mingled rays
Of suns that know no winter days?

Reason indeed may oft complain
For Nature's sad reality,
And tell the suffering heart how vain
Its cherished dreams must always be;
And Truth may rudely trample down
The flowers of Fancy newly blown.

But thou art ever there to bring
The hovering vision back, and breathe
New glories o'er the blighted spring
And call a lovelier life from death,
And whisper with a voice divine
Of real worlds as bright as thine.

I trust not to thy phantom bliss,
Yet still in evening's quiet hour
With never-failing thankfulness
I welcome thee, benignant power,
Sure solacer of human cares
And sweeter hope, when hope despairs.

62 *Plead for Me*

Oh, thy bright eyes must answer now,
When Reason, with a scornful brow,
Is mocking at my overthrow;
O thy sweet tongue must plead for me
And tell why I have chosen thee!

Stern Reason is to judgment come
Arrayed in all her forms of gloom:
Wilt though my advocate be dumb?
No, radiant angel, speak and say
Why I did cast the world away;

Why I have persevered to shun
The common paths that others run;
And on a strange road journeyed on
Heedless alike of Wealth and Power –
Of Glory's wreath and Pleasure's flower.

These once indeed seemed Beings divine,
And they perchance heard vows of mine
And saw my offerings on their shrine –
But, careless gifts are seldom prized,
And *mine* were worthily despised.

So with a ready heart I swore
To seek their altar-stone no more;
And gave my spirit to adore
Thee, ever present, phantom thing –
My slave, my comrade, and my King!

A slave because I rule thee still;
Incline thee to my changeful will
And make thy influence good or ill –
A comrade, for by day and night
Thou art my intimate delight –

My Darling Pain that wounds and sears
And wrings a blessing out from tears
By deadening me to earthly cares;
And yet, a king – though prudence well
Have taught thy subject to rebel.

And am I wrong to worship where
Faith cannot doubt nor Hope despair
Since my own soul can grant my prayer?
Speak, God of Visions, plead for me
And tell why I have chosen thee!

63 *The Philosopher*

Enough of thought, philosopher!
Too long hast though been dreaming
Unlightened, in this chamber drear
While summer's sun is beaming –
5   Space-sweeping soul, what sad refrain
Concludes thy musings once again?

'O for the time when I shall sleep
Without identity,
And never care how rain may steep
10   Or snow may cover me!

'No promised Heaven, these wild Desires
Could all or half fulfil;
No threatened Hell, with quenchless fires,
Subdue this quenchless will!'

15   – So said I, and still say the same;
– Still to my death will say –
Three Gods within this little frame
Are warring night and day.

Heaven could not hold them all, and yet
20   They all are held in me
And must be mine till I forget
My present entity.

O for the time when in my breast
Their struggles will be o'er;
25   O for the day when I shall rest,
And never suffer more!

'I saw a Spirit standing, Man,
Where thou dost stand – an hour ago;
And round his feet, three rivers ran,
30   Of equal depth and equal flow –

'A Golden stream, and one like blood,
And one like Sapphire, seemed to be,

But where they joined their triple flood
It tumbled in an inky sea.

35 'The Spirit sent his dazzling gaze
Down through that Ocean's gloomy night,
Then – kindling all with sudden blaze,
The glad deep sparkled wide and bright –
White as the sun; far, far more fair
40 Than its divided sources were!'

And even for that Spirit, Seer,
I've watched and sought my lifetime long;
Sought Him in Heaven, Hell, Earth and Air,
An endless search – and always wrong!

45 Had I but seen his glorious eye
Once light the clouds that 'wilder me,
I ne'er had raised this coward cry
To cease to think and cease to be –

I ne'er had called oblivion blest,
50 Nor stretching eager hands to Death
Implored to change for senseless rest
This sentient soul, this living breath.

O let me die, that power and will
Their cruel strife may close,
55 And conquered good and conquering ill
Be lost in one repose.

64 *Remembrance*

Cold in the earth – and the deep snow piled above thee!
Far, far removed, cold in the dreary grave!
Have I forgot, my Only Love, to love thee,
Severed at last by Time's all-severing wave?

5 Now, when alone, do my thoughts no longer hover
Over the mountains, on that northern shore,

Resting their wings where heath and fern-leaves cover
Thy noble heart for ever, ever more?

Cold in the earth, and fifteen wild Decembers
From those brown hills, have melted into spring –
Faithful indeed is the spirit that remembers
After such years of change and suffering!

Sweet Love of youth, forgive, if I forget thee,
While the World's tide is bearing me along:
Other desires and other hopes beset me,
Hopes which obscure but cannot do thee wrong.

No later light has lightened up my heaven,
No second morn has ever shone for me;
All my life's bliss from thy dear life was given –
All my life's bliss is in the grave with thee.

But when the days of golden dreams had perished
And even Despair was powerless to destroy,
Then did I learn how existence could be cherished
Strengthened and fed without the aid of joy;

Then did I check the tears of useless passion,
Weaned my young soul from yearning after thine;
Sternly denied its burning wish to hasten
Down to that tomb already more than mine!

And even yet, I dare not let it languish,
Dare not indulge in Memory's rapturous pain;
Once drinking deep of that divinest anguish,
How could I seek the empty world again?

65 Death

Death, that struck when I was most confiding
In my certain Faith of Joy to be,
Strike again, Time's withered branch dividing
From the fresh root of Eternity!

5   Leaves, upon Time's branch, were growing brightly,
       Full of sap and full of silver dew;
       Birds, beneath its shelter, gathered nightly;
       Daily, round its flowers, the wild bees flew.

       Sorrow passed and plucked the golden blossom,
10   Guilt stripped off the foliage in its pride;
       But, within its parent's kindly bosom,
       Flowed forever Life's restoring tide.

       Little mourned I for the parted Gladness,
       For the vacant nest and silent song;
15   Hope was there and laughed me out of sadness,
       Whispering, 'Winter will not linger long.'

       And behold, with tenfold increase blessing
       Spring adorned the beauty-burdened spray;
       Wind and rain and fervent heat caressing
20   Lavished glory on that second May.

       High it rose; no wingèd grief could sweep it;
       Sin was scared to distance with its shine:
       Love and its own life had power to keep it
       From all wrong, from every blight but thine!

25   Cruel Death! The young leaves droop and languish!
       Evening's gentle air may still restore –
       No: the morning sunshine mocks my anguish –
       Time for me must never blossom more!

       Strike it down, that other boughs may flourish
30   Where that perished sapling used to be;
       Thus, at least, its mouldering corpse will nourish
       That from which it sprung – Eternity.

66 *The Visionary*

       Silent is the house: all are laid asleep;
       One, alone, looks out o'er the snow-wreaths deep;
       Watching every cloud, dreading every breeze

That whirls the wildering drift, and bends the groaning
    trees.

5 Cheerful is the hearth, soft the matted floor;
Not one shivering gust creeps through pane or door;
The little lamp burns straight, its rays shoot strong and far;
I trim it well to be the Wanderer's guiding-star.

Frown, my haughty sire; chide, my angry dame;
10 Set your slaves to spy, threaten me with shame:
But neither sire nor dame, nor prying serf shall know
What angel nightly tracks that waste of frozen snow.

What I love shall come like visitant of air,
Safe in secret power from lurking human snare;
15 Who loves me, no word of mine shall e'er betray,
Thou for faith unstained my life must forfeit pay.

Burn then, little lamp; glimmer straight and clear –
Hush! a rustling wing stirs, methinks, the air:
He for whom I wait, thus ever comes to me;
20 Strange Power! I trust thy might; trust thou my constancy.

67 *The Prisoner: a fragment*

In the dungeon-crypts idly did I stray,
Reckless of the lives wasting there away;
'Draw the ponderous bars; open, Warder stern!'
He dared not say me nay – the hinges harshly turn.

5 'Our guests are darkly lodged,' I whispered, gazing through
The vault whose grated eye showed heaven more grey than
    blue.
(This was when glad Spring laughed in awaking pride.)
'Aye, darkly lodged enough!' returned my sullen guide.

Then, God forgive my youth, forgive my careless tongue!
10 I scoffed, as the chill chains on the damp flag-stones rung;

'Confined in triple walls, art thou so much to fear,
That we must bind thee down and clench thy fetters here?'

The captive raised her face; it was as soft and mild
As sculptured marble saint or slumbering, unwean'd child;
15   It was so soft and mild, it was so sweet and fair,
Pain could not trace a line nor grief a shadow there!

The captive raised her hand and pressed it to her brow:
'I have been struck,' she said, 'and I am suffering now;
Yet these are little worth, your bolts and irons strong;
20   And were they forged in steel they could not hold me long.'

Hoarse laughed the jailor grim: 'Shall I be won to hear;
Dost think, fond dreaming wretch, that *I* shall grant thy
    prayer?
Or, better still, wilt melt my master's heart with groans?
Ah, sooner might the sun thaw down these granite stones!

25   'My master's voice is low, his aspect bland and kind,
But hard as hardest flint the soul that lurks behind;
And I am rough and rude, yet not more rough to see
Than is the hidden ghost that has its home in me!'

About her lips there played a smile of almost scorn:
30   'My friend,' she gently said, 'you have not heard me mourn;
When you my kindred's lives, *my* lost life, can restore,
Then may I weep and sue – but never, Friend, before!

'Still, let my tyrants know, I am not doomed to wear
Year after year in gloom and desolate despair;
35   A messenger of Hope comes every night to me,
And offers, for short life, eternal liberty.

'He comes with western winds, with evening's wandering
    airs,
With that clear dusk of heaven that brings the thickest stars;
Winds take a pensive tone, and stars a tender fire,
40   And visions rise, and change, that kill me with desire.

'Desire for nothing known in my maturer years
When joy grew mad with awe at counting future tears;
When, if my spirit's sky was full of flashes warm,
I knew not whence they came, from sun or thunderstorm.

45 'But first a hush of peace, a soundless calm descends;
The struggle of distress and fierce impatience ends;
Mute music soothes my breast – unuttered harmony
That I could never dream till earth was lost to me.

'Then dawns the Invisible, the Unseen its truth reveals;
50 My outward sense is gone, my inward essence feels –
Its wings are almost free, its home, its harbour found;
Measuring the gulf it stoops – and dares the final bound!

'Oh, dreadful is the check – intense the agony
When the ear begins to hear and the eye begins to see;
55 When the pulse begins to throb, the brain to think again,
The soul to feel the flesh and the flesh to feel the chain!

'Yet I would lose no sting, would wish no torture less;
The more that anguish racks the earlier it will bless;
And robed in fires of Hell, or bright with heavenly shine,
60 If it but herald Death, the vision is divine.'

She ceased to speak, and we, unanswering turned to go –
We had no further power to work the captive woe;
Her cheek, her gleaming eye, declared that man had given
A sentence unapproved, and overruled by Heaven.

68 Stanzas

Often rebuked, yet always back returning
    To those first feelings that were born with me,
And leaving busy chase of wealth and learning
    For idle dreams of things which cannot be:

5 To-day, I will seek not the shadowy region:
    Its unsustaining vastness waxes drear;

And visions rising, legion after legion,
  Bring the unreal world too strangely near.

I'll walk, but not in old heroic traces,
  10   And not in paths of high morality,
And not among the half-distinguished faces,
  The clouded forms of long-past history.

I'll walk where my own nature would be leading:
  It vexes me to choose another guide:
15 Where the gray flocks in ferny glens are feeding;
  Where the wild wind blows on the mountain side.

What have those lonely mountains worth revealing?
  More glory and more grief than I can tell:
The earth that wakes *one* human heart to feeling
  20   Can centre both the worlds of Heaven and Hell.

69 No Coward Soul

No coward soul is mine
No trembler in the world's storm-troubled sphere
I see Heaven's glories shine
And Faith shines equal arming me from Fear

5 O God within my breast
Almighty ever present Deity
Life, that in me has rest
As I Undying Life, have power in Thee.

Vain are the thousand creeds
10 That move men's hearts, unutterably vain,
Worthless as withered weeds
Or idlest froth amid the boundless main

To waken doubt in one
Holding so fast by thy infinity
15 So surely anchored on
The steadfast rock of Immortality

With wide-embracing love
Thy spirit animates eternal years
Pervades and broods above,
20   Changes, sustains, dissolves, creates, and rears.

Though Earth and moon were gone
And suns and universes ceased to be
And thou wert left alone
Every Existence would exist in thee

25   There is not room for Death
Nor atom that his might could render void
Since thou art Being and Breath
And what thou art may never be destroyed.

POEMS BY ANNE BRONTË

70 *The North Wind*

That wind is from the North: I know it well;
No other breeze could have so wild a swell.
Now deep and loud it thunders round my cell,
    Then faintly dies, and softly sighs,
5 And moans and murmurs mournfully.
I know its language: thus it speaks to me:

'I have passed over thy own mountains dear,
    Thy northern mountains, and they still are free;
Still lonely, wild, majestic, bleak, and drear,
10   And stern, and lovely, as they used to be

    'When thou, a young enthusiast,
        As wild and free as they,
O'er rocks, and glens, and snowy heights,
        Didst often love to stray.

15   'I've blown the pure, untrodden snows
    In whirling eddies from their brows;
    And I have howled in caverns wild,
    Where thou, a joyous mountain-child,
        Didst dearly love to be.
20 The sweet world is not changed, but thou
    Art pining in a dungeon now,
        Where thou must ever be.

'No voice but mine can reach thy ear,
And Heaven has kindly sent me here
25   To mourn and sigh with thee,
And tell thee of the cherished land
        Of thy nativity.'

Blow on, wild wind; thy solemn voice,
   However sad and drear,
30 Is nothing to the gloomy silence
   I have had to bear.

Hot tears are streaming from my eyes,
   But these are better far
Than that dull, gnawing, tearless time,
35   The stupor of despair.

Confined and hopeless as I am,
   Oh, speak of liberty!
Oh, tell me of my mountain home,
   And I will welcome thee!

71 *The Bluebell*

A fine and subtle spirit dwells
   In every little flower,
Each one its own sweet feeling breathes
   With more or less of power.

5 There is a silent eloquence
   In every wild bluebell,
That fills my softened heart with bliss
   That words could never tell.

Yet I recall, not long ago,
10   A bright and sunny day:
'Twas when I led a toilsome life
   So many leagues away.

That day along a sunny road
   All carelessly I strayed
15 Between two banks where smiling flowers
   Their varied hues displayed.

Before me rose a lofty hill,
   Behind me lay the sea;

My heart was not so heavy then
  As it was wont to be.

Less harassed than at other times
  I saw the scene was fair,
And spoke and laughed to those around,
  As if I knew no care.

But as I looked upon the bank,
  My wandering glances fell
Upon a little trembling flower,
  A single sweet bluebell.

Whence came that rising in my throat,
  That dimness in my eyes?
Why did those burning drops distil,
  Those bitter feelings rise?

Oh, that lone flower recalled to me
  My happy childhood's hours,
When bluebells seemed like fairy gifts,
  A prize among the flowers.

Those sunny days of merriment
  When heart and soul were free,
And when I dwelt with kindred hearts
  That loved and cared for me.

I had not then mid heartless crowds
  To spend a thankless life,
In seeking after others' weal
  With anxious toil and strife.

'Sad wanderer, weep those blissful times
  That never may return!'
The lovely floweret seemed to say,
  And thus it made me mourn.

72 *Appeal*

Oh, I am very weary,
　　Though tears no longer flow;
My eyes are tired of weeping,
　　My heart is sick of woe;

5　My life is very lonely,
　　My days pass heavily,
I'm weary of repining;
　　Wilt thou not come to me?

Oh, didst thou know my longings
10　　For thee, from day to day,
My hopes, so often blighted,
　　Thou wouldst not thus delay!

73 *Lines Written at Thorp Green*

That summer sun, whose genial glow
Now cheers my drooping spirit so,
　　Must cold and silent be,
And only light our northern clime
5　With feeble ray, before the time
　　I long so much to see.

And this soft, whispering breeze, that now
So gently cools my fevered brow,
　　This too, alas! must turn
10　To a wild blast, whose icy dart
Pierces and chills me to the heart,
　　Before I cease to mourn.

And these bright flowers I love so well,
Verbena, rose, and sweet bluebell,
15　　Must droop and die away;
Those thick, green leaves, with all their shade

And rustling music, they must fade,
   And every one decay.

But if the sunny, summer time,
20 And woods and meadows in their prime,
   Are sweet to them that roam;
Far sweeter is the winter bare,
With long, dark nights, and landscape drear,
   To them that are at Home!

74 Despondency

I have gone backward in the work,
   The labour has not sped;
Drowsy and dark my spirit lies,
   Heavy and dull as lead.

5 How can I rouse my sinking soul
   From such a lethargy?
How can I break these iron chains
   And set my spirit free?

There have been times when I have mourned
10   In anguish o'er the past,
And raised my suppliant hands on high,
   While tears fell thick and fast;

And prayed to have my sins forgiven,
   With such a fervent zeal,
15 An earnest grief, a strong desire,
   As now I cannot feel.

And vowed to trample on my sins,
   And called on Heaven to aid
My spirit in her firm resolves
20   And hear the vows I made.

And I have felt so full of love,
  So strong in spirit then,
As if my heart would never cool,
  Or wander back again.

25   And yet, alas! how many times
  My feet have gone astray!
How oft have I forgot my God!
  How greatly fallen away!

My sins increase, my love grows cold,
30   And Hope within me dies:
Even Faith itself is wavering now;
  Oh, how shall I arise?

I cannot weep, but I can pray,
  Then let me not despair;
35   Lord Jesus, save me, lest I die;
  And hear a wretch's prayer!

75 *Lines Composed in a Wood on a Windy Day*

My soul is awakened, my spirit is soaring
  And carried aloft on the wings of the breeze;
For above and around me the wild wind is roaring,
  Arousing to rapture the earth and the seas.

5   The long withered grass in the sunshine is glancing
  The bare trees are tossing their branches on high;
The dead leaves beneath them are merrily dancing,
  The white clouds are scudding across the blue sky.

I wish I could see how the ocean is lashing
10   The foam of its billows to whirlwinds of spray;
I wish I could see how its proud waves are dashing,
  And hear the wild roar of their thunder to-day!

76 *The Captive Dove*

Poor restless dove, I pity thee;
  And when I hear thy plaintive moan,
I mourn for thy captivity,
  And in thy woes forget mine own.

5   To see thee stand prepared to fly,
  And flap those useless wings of thine,
And gaze into the distant sky,
  Would melt a harder heart than mine.

In vain – in vain! Thou canst not rise:
10 Thy prison roof confines thee there;
Its slender wires delude thine eyes,
  And quench thy longings with despair.

Oh, thou wert made to wander free
  In sunny mead and shady grove,
15 And far beyond the rolling sea,
  In distant climes, at will to rove!

Yet, hadst thou but one gentle mate
  Thy little drooping heart to cheer,
And share with thee thy captive state,
20 Thou couldst be happy even there.

Yes, even there, if, listening by,
  One faithful dear companion stood;
While gazing on her full bright eye,
  Thou mightst forget thy native wood.

25 But thou, poor solitary dove,
  Must make, unheard, thy joyless moan;
The heart that Nature formed to love
  Must pine, neglected, and alone.

77 *The Consolation*

Though bleak these woods, and damp the ground
    With fallen leaves so thickly strown,
And cold the wind that wanders round
    With wild and melancholy moan;

5   There *is* a friendly roof I know,
        Might shield me from the wintry blast;
    There is a fire, whose ruddy glow
        Will cheer me for my wanderings past.

    And so, though still, where'er I go,
10   Cold stranger-glances meet my eye;
    Though, when my spirit sinks in woe,
        Unheeded swells the unbidden sigh;

    Though solitude, endured too long,
        Bids youthful joys too soon decay,
15 Makes mirth a stranger to my tongue,
        And overclouds my noon of day;

    When kindly thoughts that would have way,
        Flow back discouraged to my breast;
    I know there *is*, though far away,
20   A home where heart and soul may rest.

    Warm hands are there, that, clasped in mine,
        The warmer heart will not belie;
    While mirth, and truth, and friendship shine
        In smiling lip and earnest eye.

25 The ice that gathers round my heart
        May there be thawed; and sweetly, then,
    The joys of youth, that now depart,
        Will come to cheer my soul again.

    Though far I roam, that thought shall be
        My hope, my comfort, everywhere;
    While such a home remains to me,
        My heart shall never know despair!

78 *Past Days*

'Tis strange to think there *was* a time
　　When mirth was not an empty name,
When laughter really cheered the heart,
　　And frequent smiles unbidden came,
5　And tears of grief would only flow
　　In sympathy for others' woe;

When speech expressed the inward thought,
　　And heart to kindred heart was bare,
And summer days were far too short
10　　For all the pleasures crowded there;
And silence, solitude, and rest, –
Now welcome to the weary breast –

Were all unprized, uncourted then;
　　And all the joy one spirit showed,
15　The other deeply felt again;
　　And friendship like a river flowed,
Constant and strong its silent course,
For nought withstood its gentle force:

When night, the holy time of peace,
20　　Was dreaded as the parting hour;
When speech and mirth at once must cease,
　　And silence must resume her power;
Though ever free from pains and woes,
She only brought us calm repose.

25　And when the blessed dawn again
　　Brought daylight to the blushing skies,
We woke, and not *reluctant* then,
　　To joyless *labour* did we rise;
But full of hope, and glad and gay,
30　We welcomed the returning day.

79 *A Reminiscence*

Yes, thou art gone! and never more
    Thy sunny smile shall gladden me;
But I may pass the old church door,
    And pace the floor that covers thee,

5   May stand upon the cold, damp stone,
    And think that, frozen, lies below
The lightest heart that I have known,
    The kindest I shall ever know.

Yet, though I cannot see thee more,
10   'Tis still a comfort to have seen;
And though thy transient life is o'er,
    'Tis sweet to think that thou hast been;

To think a soul so near divine,
    Within a form so angel fair,
15 United to a heart like thine,
    Has gladdened once our humble sphere.

80 *Music on Christmas Morning*

Music I love – but never strain
    Could kindle raptures so divine,
So grief assuage, so conquer pain,
    And rouse this pensive heart of mine –
5   As that we hear on Christmas morn
Upon the wintry breezes borne.

Though Darkness still her empire keep,
    And hours must pass, ere morning break;
From troubled dreams, or slumbers deep,
10   That music *kindly* bids us wake:
It calls us, with an angel's voice,
To wake, and worship, and rejoice;

To greet with joy the glorious morn,
　　Which angels welcomed long ago,
15　When our redeeming Lord was born,
　　To bring the light of Heaven below;
The Powers of Darkness to dispel,
And rescue Earth from Death and Hell.

While listening to that sacred strain,
20　　My raptured spirit soars on high;
I seem to hear those songs again
　　Resounding through the open sky,
That kindled such divine delight,
In those who watched their flocks by night.

25　With them, I celebrate His birth –
　　Glory to God in highest Heaven,
Good-will to men, and peace on earth,
　　To us a Saviour-king is given;
Our God is come to claim His own,
30　And Satan's power is overthrown!

A sinless God, for sinful men,
　　Descends to suffer and to bleed;
Hell *must* renounce its empire then;
　　The price is paid, the world is freed,
35　And Satan's self must now confess
That Christ has earned a *Right* to bless:

Now holy Peace may smile from Heaven,
　　And heavenly Truth from earth shall spring:
The captive's galling bonds are riven,
40　　For our Redeemer is our King;
And He that gave His blood for men
Will lead us home to God again.

81 Night

I love the silent hour of night,
  For blissful dreams may then arise,
Revealing to my charmèd sight
  What may not bless my waking eyes.

5 And then a voice may meet my ear,
  That death has silenced long ago;
And hope and rapture may appear
  Instead of solitude and woe.

Cold in the grave for years has lain
10 The form it was my bliss to see;
And only dreams can bring again
  The darling of my heart to me.

82 Home

How brightly glistening in the sun
  The woodland ivy plays!
While yonder beeches from their barks
  Reflect his silver rays.

5 That sun surveys a lovely scene
  From softly smiling skies;
And wildly through unnumbered trees
  The wind of winter sighs:

Now loud, it thunders o'er my head,
10 And now in distance dies.
But give me back my barren hills
  Where colder breezes rise;

Where scarce the scattered, stunted trees
  Can yield an answering swell,
15 But where a wilderness of heath
  Returns the sound as well.

For yonder garden, fair and wide,
  With groves of evergreen,
Long winding walks, and borders trim,
20   And velvet lawns between –

Restore to me that little spot,
  With grey walls compassed round,
Where knotted grass neglected lies,
  And weeds usurp the ground.

25 Though all around this mansion high
   Invites the foot to roam,
And though its halls are fair within –
  Oh, give me back my HOME!

83 If This Be All

O God! if this indeed be all
  That Life can show to me;
If on my aching brow may fall
  No freshening dew from Thee;

5 If with no brighter light than this
  The lamp of hope may glow
And I may only *dream* of bliss,
  And wake to weary woe;

If friendship's solace must decay,
10   When other joys are gone,
And love must keep so far away,
  While I go wandering on, –

Wandering and toiling without gain,
  The slave of others' will,
15 With constant care and frequent pain,
  Despised, forgotten still;

Grieving to look on vice and sin,
  Yet powerless to quell

The silent current from within,
    The outward torrent's swell;

While all the good I would impart,
    The feelings I would share,
Are driven backward to my heart,
    And turned to wormwood there;

If clouds must *ever* keep from sight
    The glories of the Sun,
And I must suffer Winter's blight,
    Ere Summer is begun:

If Life must be so full of care –
    Then call me soon to Thee;
Or give me strength enough to bear
    My load of misery.

84 'Oh, they have robbed me of the hope'

Oh, they have robbed me of the hope
    My spirit held so dear;
They will not let me hear that voice
    My soul delights to hear.

They will not let me see that face
    I so delight to see;
And they have taken all thy smiles,
    And all thy love from me.

Well, let them seize on all they can; –
    One treasure still is mine, –
A heart that loves to think on thee,
    And feels the worth of thine.

85 'Farewell to thee'

Farewell to thee! but not farewell
    To all my fondest thoughts of thee:

Within my heart they still shall dwell;
　　And they shall cheer and comfort me.

5　　O beautiful, and full of grace!
　　If thou hadst never met mine eye,
I had not dreamed a living face
　　Could fancied charms so far outvie.

If I may ne'er behold again
10　　That form and face so dear to me,
Nor hear thy voice, still would I fain
　　Preserve for aye their memory.

That voice, the magic of whose tone
　　Could wake an echo in my breast,
15　Creating feelings that, alone,
　　Can make my trancèd spirit blest.

That laughing eye, whose sunny beam
　　My memory would not cherish less; –
And oh, that smile! whose joyous gleam
20　　No mortal language can express.

Adieu! but let me cherish still
　　The hope with which I cannot part.
Contempt may wound, and coldness chill,
　　But still it lingers in my heart.

25　And who can tell but Heaven, at last,
　　May answer all my thousand prayers,
And bid the future pay the past
　　With joy for anguish, smiles for tears.

86 *The Narrow Way*

Believe not those who say
　　The upward path is smooth,
Lest thou shouldst stumble in the way,
　　And faint before the truth.

It is the only road
   Unto the realms of joy;
But he who seeks that blest abode
   Must all his powers employ.

Bright hopes and pure delights
   Upon his course may beam,
And there, amid the sternest heights,
   The sweetest flowerets gleam.

On all her breezes borne,
   Earth yields no scents like those;
But he that dares not grasp the thorn
   Should never crave the rose.

Arm – arm thee for the fight!
   Cast useless loads away;
Watch through the darkest hours of night,
   Toil through the hottest day.

Crush pride into the dust,
   Or thou must needs be slack;
And trample down rebellious lust,
   Or it will hold thee back.

Seek not thy honour here;
   Waive pleasure and renown;
The world's dread scoff undaunted bear,
   And face its deadliest frown.

To labour and to love,
   To pardon and endure,
To lift thy heart to God above,
   And keep thy conscience pure;

Be this thy constant aim,
   Thy hope, thy chief delight;
What matter who should whisper blame,
   Or who should scorn or slight?

What matter, if thy God approve,
    And if, within thy breast,
Thou feel the comfort of His love,
40   The earnest of His rest?

87 *Last Lines*

A dreadful darkness closes in
    On my bewildered mind;
O let me suffer and not sin,
    Be tortured yet resigned.

5   Through all this world of blinding mist
    Still let me look to thee,
And give me courage to resist
    The Tempter, till he flee.

Weary I am – O give me strength,
10   And leave me not to faint:
Say thou wilt comfort me at length
    And pity my complaint.

I've begged to serve thee heart and soul,
    To sacrifice to Thee
15 No niggard portion, but the whole
    Of my identity.

I hoped amid the brave and strong
    My portioned task might lie,
To toil amid the labouring throng
20   With purpose keen and high;

But thou hast fixed another part,
    And thou hast fixed it well;
I said so with my breaking heart
    When first the anguish fell.

25 O thou hast taken my delight
    And hope of life away,
And bid me watch the painful night
    And wait the weary day.

The hope and the delight were thine:
   I bless thee for their loan;
30   I gave thee while I deemed them mine
   Too little thanks, I own.

Shall I with joy thy blessings share
   And not endure their loss;
35   Or hope the martyr's crown to wear
   And cast away the cross?

These weary hours will not be lost,
   These days of passive misery,
These nights of darkness, anguish-tost,
40   If I can fix my heart on thee.

The wretch that weak and weary lies
   Crushed with sorrow, worn with pain,
Still to Heaven may lift his eyes
   And strive and labour not in vain;

45 Weak and weary though I lie
   Crushed with sorrow, worn with pain,
I may lift to Heaven mine eye
   And strive and labour not in vain;

That inward strife against the sins
50   That ever wait on suffering
To strike wherever first begins
   Each ill that would corruption bring;

That secret labour to sustain
   With humble patience every blow;
55 To gather fortitude from pain
   And hope and holiness from woe.

Thus let me serve thee from my heart
   Whate'er may be my written fate,
Whether thus early to depart
60   Or yet a while to wait.

If thou shouldst bring me back to life,
　　More humbled I should be,
More wise, more strengthened for the strife,
　　More apt to lean on thee.

65　　Should Death be standing at the gate,
　　Thus should I keep my vow;
But hard whate'er my future fate,
　　So let me serve thee now.

NOTES

1 **Lines on Seeing the Portrait of . . . Painted by De Lisle** (10 November 1830). One of Charlotte's Glasstown poems, written at the age of fourteen, in the character of Arthur Wellesley, Marquis of Douro, who is described as 'member of the society of antiquarians, president for 1830 of the Literary Club; Honorary Member of the academy of artists and treasurer to the society for the spread of classical knowledge; chief secretary of the confederate hundred for promoting gymnastic exercises'. Sir Edward (sometimes called Frederick) De Lisle was one of the artists patronised by the Marquis and had just painted a portrait of Douro's childhood sweetheart and fiancée Marion Hume, as Hebe, the female cupbearer to the gods and wife of Hercules in classical mythology. Marion herself was the naive, innocent heroine of Glasstown who was always symbolically dressed simply and in white. Here her portrait inspires her fiancé to lyrical praise. Though the lines are by no means perfect, they reflect Charlotte's remarkable breadth of reading and they are firmly in the literary tradition of 'Lines on the portrait of . . .'.

2 **Marion's Song** (20 August 1832). A second poem from the Glasstown sagas, again relating to Marion Hume. This time, however, she is not the subject but rather the mouthpiece of the poem: the lines are a song sung to the accompaniment of a little ivory lyre by the newly wedded Marion to her bridegroom, the Marquis of Douro. The song itself was one that Marion had sung the evening before Douro had left her during their engagement, and in that context it appears to have taken the form of a prayer for Douro's safety and sure return to her. The ominous note in the last two lines foreshadows the tragedies that are to follow. In *The Bridal*, the version of their story to which this poem belongs, Douro was almost tricked into marrying Lady Zenobia Ellrington but was saved by a friendly spirit and returned in triumph to claim his bride. In other versions, however, Marion was abandoned and died of a broken heart, or later died of consumption neglected by her husband. The splendidly sonorous opening lines of the song are particularly reminiscent of the Psalms, with which Charlotte was familiar, echoing their elegiac mood and metre.

3 **Lines on Bewick** (27 November 1832). The influence of Thomas Bewick (1753–1828), the wood engraver whose illustrations for children's books and, more particularly, for a *History of British Birds* made him famous, was very marked on the Brontës. They owned a copy of the *British Birds* and as children most if not all their earliest extant drawings were copies from Bewick woodcuts: the loving

detail with which Branwell copied the snarling farmyard dog, Charlotte the cormorant on the stormy seashore and Emily the peasant woman herding geese reflect the fascination which his vignettes had for imaginative children. Two years after she wrote this eulogy, Charlotte recommended Bewick as valuable reading on the subject of natural history to Ellen Nussey (L. & L., i, 111). This poem, graphically describing Bewick's vignettes, is best paralleled in the first chapter of *Jane Eyre*. The lonely child Jane, wishing to escape from her sadistic cousin, found refuge in a window seat and the study of Bewick's *British Birds*. The text she mainly passed over, though the descriptions of Scandinavia had some appeal:

> The words in these introductory pages connected themselves with the succeeding vignettes, and gave significance to the rock standing up alone in a sea of billow and spray; to the broken boat stranded on a desolate coast; to the cold and ghastly moon glancing through bars of cloud at a wreck just sinking.
>
> I cannot tell what sentiment haunted the quite solitary churchyard, with its inscribed headstone; its gate, its two trees, its low horizon, girdled by a broken wall, and its newly-risen crescent, attesting the hour of even-tide.
>
> The two ships becalmed on a torpid sea, I believed to be marine phantoms.
>
> The fiend pinning down the thief's pack behind him, I passed over quickly: it was an object of terror.
>
> So was the black, horned thing seated aloof on a rock, surveying a distant crowd surrounding a gallows.
>
> Each picture told a story; mysterious often to my undeveloped understanding and imperfect feelings, yet ever profoundly interesting . . .
>
> With Bewick on my knee, I was then happy: happy at least in my way.

4 A National Ode for the Angrians (17 July 1843). The kingdom of Angria was founded some time in the winter of 1833 by Branwell and Charlotte. It lay to the east of Glasstown and was a flat land divided by four rivers, acquired by conquest under the leadership of Arthur Wellesley, now Duke of Zamorna. The grateful citizens of Glasstown, at his request, conferred the kingdom of Angria upon him and the country was divided into seven provinces each with its own capital and its own lord lieutenant. The new land was carefully mapped out and Charlotte's poem draws heavily on Branwell's detailed census of the area, which listed the population and names of the capitals and lord lieutenants of each province. Written in the first few months of the new kingdom's foundation, the poem is a battle hymn for Angria purportedly written by Zamorna; its militaristic rhythm effectively echoes the martial character of Zamorna and the call to arms which it includes. The listing of resonant names is typical of classical poetry which the Brontës studied, and the inclusion of many Scottish names reflects the Brontës' love of border ballads and the novels of Walter Scott.

1 **Calabar** Angrian province, 190 miles by 150 miles, whose capital was Gazemba. Also one of the four rivers of Angria.

3 **Etrei** Angrian province, 120 miles by 95 miles, whose capital was Dongola.

4 **Northangerland** the largest province of Angria, 200 miles by 270 miles, whose

capital was Pequene. Its lord lieutenant, Alexander Percy, was to become Zamorna's arch-enemy.

5 Zamorna   the most populous province of Angria, 170 miles by 112 miles, whose capital was Zamorna.

6 Enna   unidentified.

7 Angria   province which gave its name to the kingdom, 80 miles by 180 miles, whose capital was also called Angria.

9–11 Romalla ... Pendlebrow ... Boulsworth   mountains of Angria.

12–13 Hawkscliffe   ancient forests in the Sydenham hills, where Zamorna's mistress, Mina Laury, lived.

15 Edwardston   country estate of Edward Percy, scene of Zamorna's defeat in battle against the Reform Ministry of Glasstown.

16 Olympia   river of Angria, on whose banks Edward Percy constructed great manufacturing mills.

17 Arundel   Angrian province, 165 miles by 90 miles whose capital was Seaton.

18 Guadima   river of Angria.

25 Enara   General Henri Fernando Di Enara, lord lieutenant of Etrei provence, an Italian commander in chief of the Angrian forces, loyal to Zamorna.

26 Warner   Warner Howard Warner, lord lieutenant of Angria province, who later became Prime Minister of the kingdom; head of a large and important family and valuable ally of Zamorna.

27 Howard   John Howard, a member of the Warner clan.

29 Gor-cock   Scottish and northern English dialect term for the male red grouse.

29–32 Agar ... Moray ... Southwood   unidentified.

33 Segovia   Maria (Augusta) di Segovia, a wicked Italian, first wife of Alexander Percy, poisoned by her accomplices for withholding payment for their murder of her father-in-law.

34 Chevalier of Arundel   Viscount Frederick Lofty, earl of Arundel, friend and general of Zamorna, lord lieutenant of Arundel province and Grand Chamberlain of Angria.

39 Percy   Alexander Percy, duke of Northangerland, lord lieutenant of Northangerland province; evil genius of Angria whose political and military struggles against Zamorna form the basis of the Angrian chronicles. At this early period, however, he is an ally of Zamorna.

44 Aornus   mountain of Angria.

45 son of that tremendous sire: Edward Percy, disowned elder son of Northangerland who was 'a first rate Angrian as to appearance', despite being one of the leading industrialists of the new kingdom.

56 Afric's   Angria, like Glasstown, was an African kingdom despite its typically British climate and countryside.

5 Retrospection (19 December 1835). These twelve lines are from the beginning of a much longer poem which has a continuation in prose. It was written at the age of nineteen, when Charlotte was a teacher at Miss Wooler's school at Roe

Head, and it reveals just how important and necessary to her the world of Angria had become. From early childhood, with the invention of the Glasstown sagas, Angria had been a source of delight, excitement and solace; now, in exile from home and Branwell, her chief playing partner, and having just begun to earn her own living in an uncongenial occupation, Angria became not merely a refuge but a necessary prop to her existence. These lines refer to the inception of the 'bright, darling dream' which had such small beginnings and which could not have been expected to continue beyond childhood. The questions in lines 8–10 are purely rhetorical, for in the continuation of the poem Charlotte makes it perfectly clear that Angria is not only alive and well but flourishing.

6 **Stanzas** (14 May 1837). Charlotte evidently considered this one of her better Angrian poems. It was written while she was teaching at Roe Head, but she copied it up again at Haworth on 30 August 1845 and then published it in the sisters' volume of poems in 1846. Like many of her sisters' Gondal poems, these lines are in the first person and are on the subject of separation. The speaker is an abandoned lover who, in the manner typical of most of Charlotte's heroines, remains passive and faithful to the end, despite being deserted and maltreated. The poem conjures up in lyric terms the times when memories of her might be evoked in her lover's mind and goes on to express the hope that he might, just once, even if it were after her death, show some lingering tenderness for her.

Text: 1846.

7 **The Teacher's Monologue** (15 May 1837). This poem, published in 1846 under the title 'The Teacher's Monologue', was written at Roe Head, only a day after no. 6. This time, however, the lines are much more personal and do not immediately relate to Angria. Like Emily and Anne, Charlotte suffered intensely from homesickness (lines 11–12); it was not merely the separation from those she loved that she found so trying but also, and more importantly, the restrictions on her mental and physical liberty which she could only freely indulge at home – where her time was her own and she had the sympathetic and stimulating companionship of her family. The monotony of teaching which demanded so large a part of her time left her embittered and despondent as to her future prospects. Despite the apparent resignation to her lot in lines 87–8 it is evident that Charlotte's ambitious spirit was still chafing. Only two months before, she had received Southey's crushing reply telling her: 'The day dreams in which you habitually indulge are likely to induce a distempered state of mind; and, in proportion as all the ordinary uses of the world seem to you flat and unprofitable, you will be unfitted for them without becoming fitted for anything else.' (L. & L., i, 128.) No doubt Charlotte had taken these words to heart, hence her mood of disillusionment and hopelessness at the prospect of a lifetime in an uncongenial career.

Text: 1846.

8 **Parting** (29 January 1838). A personal poem, written on the last day of the Christmas holidays before Charlotte's return to Miss Wooler's school which had

just removed from Roe Head to Dewsbury Moor. The mood is one of enforced cheerfulness; Charlotte reminds her sisters (and herself as much as anybody) that physical separation cannot break the bonds of common memory and mutual thoughts. Charlotte made a fair copy of the poem while she was in Brussels in 1843 when the sentiments must have again seemed very appropriate for she was separated from the family, this time even further away than before. In 1846 Charlotte published the poem in the sisters' volume of poetry and in 1853 it was set to music and republished by J.E. Field of London.

Text: 1846.

9 Life (26 March 1839). This poem appears on the last page of one of Charlotte's juvenile works, *Henry Hastings*. It was fair-copied at Brussels in 1843 when Charlotte appears to have been collecting and reworking many of her earlier poems and was then published in 1846 under the title 'Life'. The unusually optimistic tone of the poem was perhaps partly induced by the fact that it was written at home at a time when all the family were together, except for Branwell who was apparently making a living as a portrait painter in Bradford. Charlotte herself had given up her position at Miss Wooler's school, disliking its new location, Emily had just returned from a teaching post at Law Hill and Anne had just ended her own schooling at Miss Wooler's. Within a couple of months, Charlotte and Anne would have new positions as governesses and Branwell would have returned home in debt; the poem therefore falls in a tranquil interlude. No doubt it also reflects the gaiety of its supposed author, Charles Townshend, a cynical observer of Angrian society.

Text: 1846.

10 A Valentine (February 1840). This light-hearted poem was written by Charlotte with the aid of Emily and Anne, and of Ellen Nussey who was staying with them at the time, and was addressed to the Reverend William Weightman, Mr Brontë's new curate. Mr Weightman was kind, generous and constitutionally cheerful: as such he was a welcome addition to the family circle at Haworth Parsonage. When he learnt that none of the girls had ever received a valentine, he walked all the way to Bradford and back to post them one each. He had written personally addressed verses for each valentine, three of which Ellen remembered in later life as being entitled 'Fair Ellen, Fair Ellen', 'Away, Fond Love' and 'Soul Divine'. The girls responded in similar vein, though Charlotte (who was apparently quite smitten with Mr Weightman's charms) took the lead. Their valentine acknowledged Mr Weightman's worth and the inevitability of his travelling on to greater and more glorious things than the moorland curacy of Haworth: ironically, however, he never left Haworth, for he caught cholera while visiting the parish sick and died of the disease in September 1842. By that time Charlotte had changed her opinion of him, having had the opportunity of observing his numerous flirtations. On 3 March 1841 she wrote to Ellen Nussey: 'I dare say you have received a valentine this year from our bonny-faced friend the curate of Haworth. I got a precious specimen a few days before I left home, but I knew better how to treat it than I did those we received a year ago . . . I

honour and admire his generous, open disposition, and sweet temper – but for all the tricks, wiles, and insincerities of love the gentleman has not his match for twenty miles round. He would fain persuade every woman under thirty whom he sees that he is desperately in love with her.' [L. & L., i, 204–6.]

1 **A Roland for your Oliver** a tit for tat, referring to the evenly matched combat between Roland and Oliver, paladins of Charlemagne, which was the origin of their friendship.

21–2 **A stranger and a pilgrim** Weightman was a native of Appleby in Cumbria, and a graduate of Durham University.

11 **Passion** (12 December 1841). One of Charlotte's better poems, adopting the simpler vocabulary used by her sisters in preference to her usually archaic choice of metre and language. It is one of the most interesting examples of how Charlotte re-edited her material. Originally, the poem had a Peninsular War setting. Wellington, who made his name in the Peninsular War, had always been the hero of the Brontë family and the twelve toy soldiers whose imaginary adventures were the beginning of the Glasstown and Angrian sagas were supposed to be veterans of his armies. By 1846, however, Wellington's campaigns in Spain and Portugal were no longer relevant except to the Brontës' Angrian world and the Sikh wars in India were much more topical. In November 1845 the Sikhs in the Punjab declared war and at the time when the sisters were sending their completed manuscript to Aylott and Jones in early 1846 the British, against all odds and with very heavy casualties, were winning several battles culminating in the great victories of Aliwal on 28 January 1846 and Sobraon on the Sutlej river on 10 February 1846. The updated references to the Sikh wars could hardly have been more topical. The poem clearly began in an Angrian context; the poet defies his lover to withhold her love if he returns a hero from the wars; his sufferings will move her pity, his glory will awaken her pride.

Text: 1846. For the manuscript variants see Victor Neufeldt, *The Poems of Charlotte Brontë* (Garland Publishing, 1985), pp.480–1.

19 **Seik** archaic spelling of Sikh.

20–21 **Sutlej** a tributary of the Indus, forming the southernmost boundary of the Sikh Punjab.

12 **Evening Solace** (undated, but first published in 1846). A rueful yet resigned poem which Charlotte published in 1846 under the title 'Evening Solace'. The opening lines aptly summarize Charlotte's feelings about Angria, part of whose potency lay in the fact that it was a secret world 'Whose charms were broken if revealed' (line 4). The poem reworks a commonplace idea: the soothing effect of the passage of time which turns the sufferings of past experience into memories which can be recalled in tranquillity with only a lingering sense of melancholy. The subject is treated in a sympathetic manner, however, and the poem contains some of Charlotte's best lines, partly because here she has abandoned her usual deliberately archaic, poetic vocabulary. The lines, 'When soft as birds their pinions closing,/The heart's best feelings gather home', are particularly felicitous. There

are some similarities here with Emily's poem, 'I am the only being whose doom' (no. 38).

Text: 1846.

1–2 Compare with Emily, no. 38, lines 5–6.

13 'He saw my heart's woe' (undated, but the manuscript of this poem appears on the back of a letter to W.S. Williams, the proof-reader at Smith, Elder and Co., dated 13 November 1847). This personal poem, which appears to date from 1847 or even later, relates to Charlotte's formative experiences in Brussels in 1842–3. Whether she fell in love with her married tutor, Monsieur Heger, or whether she simply made him an object of extreme hero-worship because of his appreciation of her talents is, to a certain extent, irrelevant. Whatever its nature, the relationship inspired a considerable output on the subject of master-pupil relations, including two novels, *The Professor* (published posthumously in 1857) and *Villette* (1853), and a large number of poems. These lines, though they do not overtly mention this type of situation, have great relevance to Charlotte's own experience. Like Monsieur Heger, the idol/master of the peom perceived his pupil's admiration and responded by ignoring it in the hopes that this would end her infatuation. He prohibited Charlotte from writing to him more than once every six months (though there are indications that she wrote more often) and her pathetic letters begging for even the shortest of replies are paralleled in the second verse of the poem, where the idolater annually appeals for aid, 'entreating some reply'. Similarly, Monsieur Heger's determined silence and Charlotte's own refusal to accept another teaching post after her return from Brussels are echoed in the granite imperturbability of the idolised one and the idolater's withdrawal 'to an exile from my kind' (line 18). In the poem, however, the self-loathing is only overcome by the knowledge of God's forgiveness while, for Charlotte, the feelings of guilt and shame were eventually exorcised through the cathartic effect of writing.

16 Baal   a false god, often a graven image worshipped for magical powers.

14 On the Death of Emily Jane Brontë (24 December [1848]). Emily Brontë died suddenly on 19 December 1848, less than three months after her brother Branwell. Though the family had suspected the fatal nature of her consumption Emily had refused to see a doctor or even admit that she was ill, carrying on with her normal household tasks by means of her 'indomitable will' alone. On the very day she died Charlotte had written to Ellen Nussey saying that there was no hope, but she little suspected that Emily was to die that very afternoon, fighting for life with her last breath. This poem was written two days after the funeral: the next day Charlotte expressed similar feelings in her letter to W.S. Williams: 'some sad comfort I take, as I hear the wind blow and feel the cutting keenness of the frost, in knowing that the elements bring her no more suffering; their severity cannot reach her grave; her fever is quieted, her restlessness soothed, her deep, hollow cough is hushed for ever; we do not hear it in the night nor listen for it in the

morning; we have not the conflict of the strangely strong spirit and the fragile frame before us – relentless conflict – once seen, never to be forgotten . . . I will not now ask why Emily was torn from us in the fulness of our attachment, rooted up in the prime of her own days, in the promise of her powers; why her existence now lies like a field of green corn trodden down, like a tree in full bearing struck at the root. I will only say, sweet is rest after labour and calm after tempest, and repeat again and again that Emily knows that now.' (L. & L., ii, 16–17.)

15 **On the Death of Anne Brontë** (31 June 1849). During the first week of January 1849, less than a fortnight after Emily's death, Anne was diagnosed as consumptive. At first there was some hope of recovery because the disease was not too far advanced and Anne submitted patiently to all the doctor's battery of pills, plasters and medicines – if only to comfort Charlotte who had been unable to do anything for Emily. In May 1849 she went to Scarborough, accompanied by Charlotte and Ellen Nussey, in the vain hope of a sea-cure; there she died and was buried, at her own request, in St Mary's churchyard to save her father the trauma of a third funeral in nine months. This poem was written just over a month after Anne's death when Charlotte had returned to the Parsonage. The tone of resignation is more sincere and more pronounced here than in her poem on Emily's death (no. 14) but this reflects Charlotte's own attitude. On 4 June 1849 she had written to W.S. Williams contrasting the deaths of her two sisters; Anne's quiet Christian end, trusting in a future life, which seemed to fulfil all Charlotte's forebodings of an early death for her and, on the other hand, Emily's desperate struggle against death and untimely uprooting from life. Compare this poem with Anne's own reaction to the news of the fatal nature of her illness (no. 87).

16 **Augusta** (spring 1834). This poem was apparently written shortly after the foundation of the kingdom of Angria, when the Glasstown sagas had been 'played out' and a new impetus was needed to revive flagging enthusiasm. It appears in a prose life of Alexander Percy, Branwell's favourite character, and the lines purport to be written by him. They are addressed to Augusta (Maria) di Segovia, an Italian beauty who seduced the teenage Percy into marriage knowing him to be a wealthy heir. Later, she hired several villains to murder her father-in-law so that Percy would inherit his estates, but when she withheld their payment they poisoned her. This poem pre-dates these events, however; the young Percy is supposed to have written it in 1812 when he was on the Philosopher's Isle. The Isle was the site of a college founded for the compulsory training and education of the noble youths of Glasstown and its subterranean caves provided prisons for the punishment of the indolent and stupid. The island location of the college explains the seas which divide Percy and Augusta in the poem and provides the setting for a remarkably evocative description of a moonlit sky (lines 9–32). These lines are not purposeless description, however, for they lead the poet to compare the changing scene with the chaos in his own soul and to contrast the borrowed light of the moon with Augusta's own beauty.

17 **The Doubter's Hymn** ((November 1835). These lines, which compare

favourably with some of Emily's best, were written by Branwell as part of his book on the Angrian hero, Alexander Percy, Earl of Northangerland. Like no. 16, they purport to have been written by Percy himself, in 1813, though the speculative, philosophical tone seems out of keeping with his character – Percy was a self-confessed atheist who refused to believe in an afterlife. Here the poet speculates on the nature of life and death and considers the possibility that, contrary to popular belief, it is life that is the sleep and death which is the awakening. It is possible that this poem was written after Branwell's first disastrous foray into the world. In July 1835 plans were afoot to send him to the Royal Academy, and Branwell himself was hoping to go in August or September; though the exact dates of his journey to London and his almost immediate return to Haworth are not known, it is possible that the whole episode already lay behind him, explaining the uncertainty expressed in the poem. Eighteen months later, while still at home, he transcribed it under the title 'The Doubter's Hymn' into a collection of his poems.

18 **Song** (17 November 1835). Another poem from the *Life of Alexander Percy*, also written in the character of the Earl of Northangerland, at about the same time as no. 17, but belonging to the year 1814 in Percy's life. Branwell transcribed the lines on 14 May 1837 into his manuscript book of poems under the title 'Song'. The poem shares the preoccupation with death and its separation of lovers which is such a feature of Emily and Anne's Gondal poetry. It is not entirely clear which of Percy's many wives and mistresses is here being mourned.

19 **Memory** (July 1836). A short poem by Branwell which was attributed to Emily by Clement Shorter when he published a facsimile of the manuscript in his *Complete Works of Emily Jame Brontë* (Hodder & Stoughton, 1910), i (prose), 446. On this draft, which he later reworked several times, Branwell wrote: 'I am more terrifically and infernally and Idiotically and Brutally STUPID – than ever I was in the whole course of my incarnate existence. The above precious lines are the fruits of one hour's most agonising labour between ½ past 6 and ½ past 7 in the evening of Wednesday July 1836.' The poem appears to belong to the Angrian cycle; the character into whose mouth the poem is put has become an insensate being unable to feel emotion. Eventually the power of memory revives him, sweeping over his heart-strings as if over the strings of a harp. In December 1835 and again in April 1836 Branwell had written to *Blackwood's Magazine* sending samples of his work, so it is possible that the different drafts of this poem were written with an eye to publication.

11 **Eolian** Aeolus, god of the winds, gave Odysseus a bag containing all the winds unfavourable to his voyage. Out of curiosity, his sailors opened the bag, thereby releasing the winds and causing their ship to be driven back by storms.

20 **Mary's Prayer** (16 June 1837). This short but evocative poem belongs to the Angrian cycle. It has many similarities in form, style and subject with Emily's poems 'Song' (no. 60) and 'Remembrance' (no. 64), and Anne's poem 'A Reminiscence' (no. 79), though here it is the dying character not the mourner,

who speaks. This reworking of similar themes reveals how interdependent the worlds of Angria and Gondal were and how the Brontës were stimulated to write by the interchange of ideas. Here Branwell is writing in the character of Mary Percy, though it is not clear whether this is Northangerland's wife or daughter, since both led unhappy lives. It is more likely to be the daughter who, as wife of Zamorna, was the unfortunate pawn in the quarrels between Angria's two arch-heroes. As she was loved by both father and husband, the best way for each to attack the other was to hurt her, and eventually she died broken-hearted in exile at Alnwick, victim of their hatred. The economy of language employed on this romantic subject prevents it sinking into sentimentality and creates a memorable poem.

21 **To Maecenas** (27 June 1840). On 1 January 1840 Branwell went to Broughton-in-Furness in Cumbria as a tutor to the Postlethwaite family. While he was there he began to translate the first book of Horace's *Odes*, producing some excellent translations which are poems in their own right. On 20 April 1840 he sent two of these to Hartley Coleridge, saying: 'the translations are two out of many made from Horace, and given to assist an answer to the question – would it be possible to obtain remuneration for translations such as those from that or any other classic author?' (L. & L., i, 182.) Branwell was thus still hoping to make a career from his poetry, though by June he had left the Postlethwaites and returned to Haworth. This poem is a translation of the first ode which Horace dedicated to his patron Maecenas and, interestingly, Branwell drew a sketch of Northangerland at the head of the manuscript, suggesting an analogy between Horace's Roman patron and Branwell's inspirational hero.

1 **sprung of kingly line**   Maecenas came from a distiguished Etruscan family and was one of the Emperor Augustus' most trusted counsellors.

12 **Lybian grain**   most of the corn consumed in Rome was imported from Libya and Sicily.

16 **Attalus**   the name of three kings of Pergamum which was proverbial for its riches.

32 **The Hunter**   the constellation Orion, named after a giant hunter of Boeotia who was placed among the stars after his death.

37 **Marsian boar**   the country of the Marsi, which lay east of Rome, was famous for wild boar.

38 **Ivy garlands**   ivy was sacred to Bacchus, the god of wine and inspiration, and thus made a suitable garland for a lyric poet like Horace or Branwell.

42 **Euterpe**   the muse of flute-playing in Greek mythology.

44 **Polyhymnia**   the muse of sacred song in Greek mythology, inventor of the lyre.

45 **Lesbian lyre**   Lesbos was the island home of Sappho and Alcaeus, two of the great Greek lyric poets imitated by Horace.

22 **To Thaliarchus** (27 June 1840). Another translation by Branwell from Horace's *Odes*, this time the one addressed to Thaliarchus, the leader of the feast (*Odes* I, ix). The poem is a drinking song for a winter party at which all thoughts

for the future are banished because youth is the time for enjoyment. The poem manages to convey the flavour of the original in an accurate translation while still maintaining a lyric quality, particularly in the first six descriptive lines. It is interesting that when Branwell reached the end of Book I of Horace's *Odes*, he did not translate the last one: on the manuscript he noted, 'This ode I have no heart to attempt, after having heard Mr H[artley] Coleridge's translation, on May day, at Ambleside.'

2 Soracte   one of the Faliscan range of hills, now called Monte Tresto, which can clearly be seen from the northern point of Rome.

10 Sabine   Branwell here follows Horace's Latin in applyingthe name of the wine to the vessel containing it. Sabine wine was neither the best nor the worst of wine and was therefore popular in ancient Rome.

23 'The desolate earth' (25 December 1841. This long poem begins, as so many of Emily's also do, with a description of the type of day Branwell was writing on. It is typical December weather which ought to depress the spirits but, on the contrary, the violence of the storms inspires Branwell to dwell on the victories of mankind achieved in the face of adverse circumstances. Galileo, Tasso, Milton, Johnson, Cowper and Burns are then cited as shining examples of men who overcame the traumas of poverty, imprisonment and physical disability to win immortality. All, incidentally, except Galileo, the Italian astronomer and physicist, were men of letters – as Branwell himself hoped to be. The poem is surprisingly optimistic in tone; the inference from the examples quoted is that Branwell still had hopes of overcoming the problems of finding fame and wealth through literature. At the time the poem was written he not only had an apparently secure job on the new Halifax railway, but was in the unusual position of having given satisfaction and having been promoted to the rank of station-master at Luddenden Foot. Branwell thus appears to be facing the prospect of a new year with confidence and optimism.

49 Galileo   Galileo Galilei (1564–1642), Italian astronomer and physicist accused of heresy and forced by the Inquisition to abjure his belief that the sun was the centre of the universe.

52 Tasso   Torquato Tasso (1544–95), Italian poet whose strange conduct, caused by constant terror of persecution, led duke Alphonso d'Este to imprison him as a madman from 1579 to 1586. Branwell is most likely to have known his story from Byron's *Lament of Tasso* in which the imprisonment is attributed to the duke's discovering that Tasso was in love with his daughter.

54 Mezentius   a cruel tyrant expelled by his people in Virgil's *Aeneid*.

55 Salem's liberty   a reference to Tasso's poem 'Jerusalem Delivered', since Salem has been identified with Jerusalem (see Genesis 14:18).

57–63   These lines refer to John Milton (1608–74), the English poet and pamphleteer who wrote many of his great works, including *Paradise Lost* and *Paradise Regained*, after he had gone blind.

77 Johnson   Dr Samuel Johnson (1709–84), English poet, essayist, journalist and lexicographer who struggled for many years against great poverty before winning fame through his *Dictionary* (1756); his reputation as a raconteur and wit rests chiefly on his portrayal in James Boswell's *Life of Johnson*.

81 Cowper   William Cowper (1731–1800), English poet who suffered severely from depression which led to periods of temporary insanity and attempted suicide; he wrote a large number of fine religious poems.

97 Burns   Robert Burns (1759–96), Scottish poet who wrote many of his best songs and verses while living in poverty and working as a farm labourer.

24 'The man who will not know another' (undated, presumably 1841–2). This poem was first published by Francis H. Grundy in his autobiography, *Pictures of the Past* (1879). Grundy was an engineer on the new Halifax railway and met Branwell when he was station-master at Luddenden Foot; the two young men were both lonely and became firm friends and drinking partners. According to Grundy, the poem originated from an occasion when Branwell 'thought I was disposed to treat him distantly at a party, and he retired in great dudgeon. When I arrived at my lodgings the same evening I found the following, necessarily an impromptu.' In fact there were already two earlier drafts of the poem, which Branwell simply altered to fit the circumstances. The poem condemns those who judge others by wealth, rank or appearance; the mind can triumph over all these disadvantages and the mind which is devoted to literature is second to none. There is some similarity of thought here with no. 23, where Branwell drew inspiration from the example of the great literary figures of the past who had won immortality despite poverty and persecution.

25 Lord Nelson (undated, *c.* 1841–2). A poem which Branwell wrote while he was station-master at Luddenden Foot: he made several drafts, the final one being entitled 'The Triumph of Mind Over Body', which aptly summarised the idea that seems to have preoccupied Branwell at this time (see nos. 23 and 24). Francis Grundy gives some interesting background on this poem: 'he wrote a poem called "Bronté", illustrative of the life of Nelson, which, at his special request, I submitted for criticism to Leigh Hunt, Miss Martineau, and others. All spoke in high terms of it. He gave it to me only about two or three weeks before his death . . .' (Grundy, *Pictures of the Past*, p.79). The poem appears to have been consciously written on a high-minded theme with an eye to publication. Nelson was a national hero, as well as being a family hero of the Brontës. (Mr Brontë, whose Irish ancestors had been called Brunty, had changed his name to Brontë when he went up to Cambridge, in direct imitation of Nelson's Sicilian title of Duke of Brontë.) This long poem is one of Branwell's best; his vignettes of Nelson's life are deftly sketched in a few rapid but vivid lines and the poem is brought to a close by a personal prayer that the poet too may share Nelson's calm courage in the face of death and danger. Perhaps surprisingly, the poem is signed 'Northangerland', reflecting Branwell's continuing obsession with his Angrian hero.

27 Nelson was only twelve years old when he first went to sea as a midshipman in 1771.

38 In 1773, aged fifteen, Nelson joined a scientific expedition to the Arctic circle sponsored by the Royal Society.

43 Mosquito shore the eastern shore of southern Mexico, Guatemala, Honduras, Nicaragua and Costa Rica: Nelson was given a command to protect this area from the depredations of American privateers in 1778–9.

44 San Juan in January 1780 Nelson commanded the naval force in an expedition up the San Juan river in Nicaragua to the Spanish stronghold of San Juan. Nelson himself nearly died of the fever he caught on this expedition.

53 Teneriffe in 1797 Nelson personally led an attack on Teneriffe and was shot just as he was stepping from the boat; his right arm was shattered and had to be amputated.

57 Copenhagen's shore in 1801 Nelson fought a battle against the Danish off Copenhagen; Nelson won a great but bloody victory, but sent the flag of truce to the king of Denmark to prevent further bloodshed.

62 Egypt's ancient flood in 1798 Nelson was sent to discover the whereabouts of the French fleet and on 1 August he discovered them lying at anchor close to the shore at Aboukir Bay. The French were unprepared and Nelson attacked with such overwhelming force that only two French frigates escaped.

63 L'Orient the largest ship of the French fleet which caught fire and exploded – the noise was heard fifteen miles away at Alexandria.

66 Aboukir the battle of the Nile was fought in Aboukir Bay.

69–74 During this battle Nelson was hit in the forehead with a piece of iron shot causing a three-inch wound in his skull. When he heard the *L'Orient* was on fire he went on deck to watch.

75 Nelson was popularly believed to have carried his coffin to battle with him, preferring not to have a conventional sea burial.

101–8 After Trafalgar, Nelson's flagship, *Victory*, was repaired and remained operational throughout the rest of the war against Napoleon; she then remained at Portsmouth throughout the latter part of the nineteenth century where she became a centre of pilgrimage.

115–16 Nelson was killed at the battle of Trafalgar on 21 October 1805.

121 wise Cornelius magician who could conjure up the past and future in his mirror.

137 old Rectory Nelson's father was parson of Burnham Thorpe in Norfolk. Branwell must have drawn an analogy between Nelson's background and his own for not only did they share a parsonage childhood but both lost their mothers at a very early age.

156 Nelson's mother died when he was nine years old.

159–78 Nelson was mortally wounded by a musket shot at the battle of Trafalgar, dying three hours later, just as victory was achieved. He spent his last hours inquiring about the progress of the battle.

177 Collingwood Cuthbert, first baron Collingwood (1750–1810), vice-admiral and lifelong friend of Nelson, who took command at Trafalgar when Nelson died. He also died at sea, in 1810, and was buried in St Paul's.

177 Trowbridge Sir Thomas Troubridge (1758–1807), rear admiral and lifelong friend of Nelson; he commanded on many of the same campaigns as Nelson and was lost at sea in 1807.

186 Westminster Nelson was in fact buried in St Paul's cathedral.

204 Hardy Sir Thomas Masterman Hardy (1769–1839), vice-admiral and friend of Nelson who fought at St Vincent, Santa Cruz and the battles of the Nile and Trafalgar; he was created first sea lord of the admiralty in 1830.

250 talents a reference to the biblical parable of the master who gave each of his servants a number of talents and rewarded those who used their initiative to increase the money (Matthew 25:14–30).

252–3 Branwell was a Tory in politics but here expresses the Whig doctrine, popularised by the *Edinburgh Review*, that progress was inevitable. The rapid advancements in political reform, economic and social sciences seemed to justify this view in the nineteenth century.

256–7 Branwell believed implicitly in his own talents – a belief which his family's fond confidence in his abilities did little to dispel. Here he seems to suggest that he might not, after all, win fame.

26 On Peaceful Death and Painful Life (undated, but published on 14 May 1842). In April 1842 Branwell was dismissed from his post as station-master at Luddenden Foot. There were unexplained irregularities in the financial accounts of the station and Branwell, as the official concerned, was held responsible, though his involvement was never proved. A month later, his pride may have been salved by the publication of this poem in *The Halifax Guardian*, a local newspaper. One of his best pieces, it treats of the seeming paradox of the happy dead for whom oblivion brings at least an absence of pain and suffering. He contrasts their lot effectively with that of the 'dead-alive' whose lives are the more hopeless because they do not believe in the prospect of a future life. The sombre tone of the poem and the bitterness of the last two lines suggest that Branwell identified himself with the 'dead-alive'; certainly, despite his parsonage upbringing, he had atheistic tendencies which deeply troubled his father.

27 'High waving heather' (13 December 1836). One of Emily's earliest preserved poems. The unusually long lines, with their strikingly insistent dactylic rhythm, are more typical of the Brontës' juvenile writings when they were experimenting with unconventional metres than of Emily's later terse style. A similar format was used by Charlotte two years earlier in her 'National Ode for the Angrians' (no. 4). The choice of rhythm here, however, may have been dictated by the subject, for the almost exultant description of the storm and flood are echoed in the exciting yet inexorable metre of the poem. This highly evocative piece is apocalyptic in tone and may, indeed, owe something to the Book of Revelations, particularly as the word 'jubilee' in line 9 is clearly used in the biblical sense of emancipation.

28 'Alone I sat' (August 1837). One of the few indications of how Emily actually composed her poetry is given in this poem. It is evening, the inspirational hour of the day for Emily, but despite the favourable circumstances and the consequent rush of ideas, the faculty of converting the inspiration into verse is denied to her on this occasion. The use of direct speech is typical of Emily's Gondal poetry even when, as in this case, the result is a soliloquy. Like many of her poems, it begins with the immediate – the precise time of composition – but because of her inability to put her thoughts into words, the poem ends abruptly and does not develop into the Gondal world.

29 'The old church tower' (October 1837). This fragment, though less finished than 'Alone I sat' (no. 28), clearly arose from similar circumstances. Again it is evening, normally the time most conducive to poetry, and Emily has seen the 'glad and glorious' day deteriorate into the gloomy rainstorms of an October evening. The immediacy of the writing is enhanced by a description of the view which Emily, waiting for inspiration, could see from the Parsonage window. The poem tails off when it becomes evident that this is a false start and is not going to lead anywhere.

30 'The night is darkening round me' (November 1837). Emily's economy of style is well displayed in this short but memorable poem. In a few words she manages to sketch a graphic picture of a snowscape and a fast descending snow storm. Despite the approaching storm and impending nightfall, the poet is held by a 'tyrant spell' which denies her all freedom of choice and prevents her seeking refuge: she 'will not, cannot go'. It is difficult to discover exactly what the 'tyrant spell' is: if Fannie Ratchford (Hatfield, *Complete Poems of Emily Jane Brontë*, p.18) is right in placing the poem in a Gondal context, then it seems likely that it relates to an incident when one of the heroines exposes her child to die on the mountains in the depths of winter. Although she cannot bear to watch the child die, as a mother she is unable to tear herself away from the place and the 'tyrant spell' is therefore her maternal emotions.

31 'I'll come when thou art saddest' (undated, but the MS is headed November 1837). This poem is untitled and nowhere is it made explicit who or what the first person narrator purports to be. From internal evidence and from comparisons with other poems (no. 61, lines 37–52) it seems likely that the visitant is imagination which, for Emily, had a mystic revelatory power. For her, the imagination was not an internal, contemplative spirit but rather, as this poem makes clear, an external, personified and independent power which could be wayward in its manifestations; it was still a personal and intensely private experience but it occurred outside her control. She was merely a passive recipient of visions and not their active creator – a view enhanced by the fact that these lines describe the recipient's emotions but through the mouth of the visitant. This poem describes the moments before the arrival of the visions: it is evening, the time most conducive to imagination's sway, and the clock has just struck the accustomed hour. The poet is alone and the air is charged with expectancy.

13–16 Compare with no. 67, lines 45–8.

32 'There are two trees' (June 1838). A short but evocative fragment preserved because it was noted down with other unfinished pieces in one of Emily's manuscript poetry books.

33 Last Words (17 October 1838). The manuscript of this poem is entitled 'Song by J. Brenzaida to G.S.'; beneath this title is written 'Love's Farewell', possibly in Charlotte's hand. Separation from a loved one through death, imprisonment, exile or, as here, through the faithlessness of one of the parties is a common theme in Gondal poetry. Julius Brenzaida, in whose character this poem is written, was Emperor of Gondal and Gaaldine. His adulterous love affair with Augusta Geraldine Almeda has been brought to a head by his demands that she leave her husband, Lord Alfred S., and marry him. When Augusta (or Geraldine as she appears here) demurred because she still loved Lord Alfred, Julius taunted her with having already betrayed him through her adultery and threatened to abandon her himself and seek solace among his former lovers. Since Julius was the great love of her life, Augusta gave in and parted from Lord Alfred, who later committed suicide.

A cautionary tale lies behind this poem. In her anxiety to prove that Emily Brontë must have had a human lover to inspire her writings, Virginia Moore transcribed the secondary title of the poem as 'Louis Parensell' and built round it a story of blighted love which was totally without foundation since it was based on a misreading of the manuscript. (V. Moore, *The Life and Eager Death of Emily Brontë*, Rich & Cowan, 1936, pp.197–207.)

Charlotte made several changes when she published the poem in 1850:
  4 slighted heart lips or heart (1850).
  5 moorside hillside (1850).
  10 rosy falsest (1850).
  14 prison strongest (1850).

34 'Light up thy halls' (1 November 1838). Gondal provides the setting for this bitter poem of parting; this time it is Fernando de Samara of Gaaldine who curses Augusta Geraldine Almeda as he is about to commit suicide. Fernando, who left his sweetheart to come to Gondal, has been seduced by Augusta, who has reverted to her former career of casual love affairs since the murder of Julius Brenzaida. Fernando's sweetheart has died broken-hearted and Fernando himself has spent some time imprisoned in the Gaaldine prison caves by Augusta. Now, alone on the moors of Gondal, he determines to free himself from his enslaving love for the treacherous Augusta in the only way possible – by killing himself.

Parallels with Fernando's love-hate relationship with Augusta are to be found in the consuming but destructive love of Catherine and Heathcliff, and many of the sentiments expressed here were later explored more fully in *Wuthering Heights*.

23–8 Compare this with *Wuthering Heights*, chapter 12, where Catherine tells Nelly Dean, 'If I were only sure it would kill him, I'd kill myself directly.'

35 Stanzas (11 November 1838). This poem probably had a Gondal setting though it was inspired by the circumstances of Emily's own life. For the first time since her brief and unhappy few months as a pupil at Roe Head school, she had left the family home, this time as a teacher at Law Hill school near Halifax. (Charlotte mistakenly attributed the composition of this, and the two following poems, nos. 36 and 37, to Emily's school days at Roe Head when she published them in 1850.) Understandably, given her reserved temperament and imaginative nature, she stood only six months of what Charlotte described as 'hard labour from six in the morning until near eleven at night, with only one half hour of exercise between' (L. & L., i, 138) before her health gave way and she returned home. This poem, beginning gloomily with a description of an unpromising November evening, is suddenly sprung to life by the hearing of a song in the distance which sends the poet into a lyrical outpouring of longing for the moorlands of home. The sight of a few 'half blighted heather bells' similarly rouses her passionate longing for the carefree liberty of former years, just as the sight of bluebell growing near Scarborough revived Anne's homesickness (no. 71) This poem ends on the hopeful note that the poet will see her beloved mountains again.

Charlotte made a large number of changes when she published this poem in 1850.
2 Through th'autumnal sky (1850).
4 Spoke of winter nigh (1850).
6–7 Did my exiled spirit grieve
   Grieved at first, but grieved not long (1850).
11 'It was spring, and the skylark was singing' (1850).
19–22 Awaken o'er all my dear moorland
       West wind, in thy glory and pride
       Oh! call me from valley and lowland
       To walk by the hill torrent's side. (1850).
25 And sullenly waves the long heather (1850).
32 In emerald and vermeil, and gold (1850).
33 **Slopes** heights (1850).
34 **glens** crags (1850).
36 **that** it (1850).
39 **dusk** dawn (1850).
42 **While** As (1850).
52 **That** Which (1850).
62 Than, for me, in that blighted heath lay (1850).
63 **that** which (1850).

36 Stanzas (4 December 1838). This poem is one of the few which can, with some confidence, be placed in a personal rather than a Gondal setting. Again, the poem was a result of Emily's employment at Law Hill: freed from the daily grind of teaching for a few hours, she is at liberty to indulge in dreams. Two ways are open to her: one is to linger on thoughts of her dearly loved home, the other is to take the more adventurous path to Gondal, and this is the one she finally chooses. The moorland scenery of Gondal is so similar to that of Haworth that the two have often been confused. There are distinct differences, however, including the more dramatic mountains and glens of the imaginary kingdom. Charlotte's substitution of the word 'sheep' for the more exotic 'deer' when she published the poem seems to be a deliberate attempt to obscure a Gondal allusion. The result of Charlotte's alterations is to make the second alternative open to the dreamer of the poem a more mundane one which, taken at face value by the uninitiated reader, could be misconstrued as simply meaning a moorland landscape in the real world.

2 The weary task is put away (1850).
4 **A little** Alike (1850). A misreading by Charlotte.
7 What spot, or near or far apart (1850).
8 **Have** Has (1850).
14 Moonless above bends twilight's dome (1850).
19 The thorn trees gaunt, the walks o'er grown (1850).
25 **Yes** Still (1850).
26 **flickering** alien (1850)
38 I knew the turfy pathway's sweep (1850).
40 **deer** sheep (1850).
44 Restraint of heavy task recoil (1850).
48 And back came labour, bondage, care (1850).

37 **The Bluebell** (18 December 1838). This poem, severely truncated by Charlotte, was published in 1850. Though the date suggests it was written during the holiday period, on internal evidence it seems to have been at least begun during Emily's brief foray into the world of the governess at Law Hill. (This is the third and the last of the three poems which Charlotte mistakenly attributed to Emily's schooldays. See nos. 35 and 36.) A winter landscape, consonant with the December date of the manuscript, is evocatively described in lines 9–16, but it is the memory of summer flowers which causes the poet to mourn the fields of home. The thought of heather, with its associations with Emily's beloved moors, is too painful to dwell on, but bluebells have a softer and more soothing spell. The description of the bluebell in lines 29–32 suggests, however, that the flower Emily had in mind was the harebell which, with its delicate stem, silvery blue flowers and slender buds, better fits her picture than the bluebell with its coarse stem and spray of dark blue flowers. This confusion is one that Anne shared for, in her poem (no. 71), she similarly described a bluebell in terms more appropriate to a harebell. For Anne too, the flower had powerful associations with home, and it is possible, given the similar themes of the two poems, that the sisters had a Gondal scenario in mind.

12 **its** her (1850).
21 **heather-bell** sweet Bluebell (1850). This change was necessitated by Charlotte's omission of the next four verses elaborating on the three flowers which had most powerful associations for Emily.
25–40 omitted (1850). The woodflower in line 25 is the violet.

42 the   that (1850).
43 the   yon (1850).
45 yearn   weep (1850).

38 'I am the only being whose doom' (17 May 1839). This poem has been seen as a personal autobiographical statement by those who have a romantic perception of Emily as an isolated and misanthropic young woman. For this reason, Hatfield 'corrected' the date of composition to 1837, so that it coincided with Emily's own eighteenth year (line 7). The manuscript, however, is clearly dated 'May 17 1839' so the poem is not autobiographical, but belongs to the Gondal cycle. The bitter and cynical tone would indeed be remarkable if it were a true reflection of Emily's own feelings at the time, but it is entirely in keeping with the dramatic emotions of Gondal. The friendless narrator of the poem, a doomed youth marked out from birth for suffering and tragedy, is a typical Gondal hero and a prototype of Heathcliff. There is, therefore, no reason to see the poem and its sentiments as a self-portrait by Emily.

1–2 Compare with *Wuthering Heights*, chapter 16, the birth of the younger Catherine: 'An unwelcomed infant it was, poor thing. It might have wailed out of life, and nobody cared a morsel, during those first hours of existence. We redeemed the neglect afterwards; but its beginning was as friendless as its end is likely to be.'

39 'And now the house-dog stretched once more' (12 July 1839). A Gondal poem, written only two months after no. 38, and featuring the same fateful character who bears such a strong resemblance to Heathcliff. The highly charged atmosphere of the poem is intensified by the contrast between the simple, homely scene of the shepherd and his family in their cottage and the almost unearthly appearance of their unexpected guest. This guest, with his black hair and strangely terrifying eyes, is probably Douglas, the outlaw who murdered the empress Augusta Geraldine Almeda, at the instigation of her stepdaughter, his lover, and who is now in flight from her avengers. Like Heathcliff, he has a mysterious, vaguely criminal past and like him, a physical presence capable of inspiring both pity and revulsion. There is also a comparison, for instance, with the passage in *Wuthering Heights*, chapter 34, where Nelly Dean confronts Heathcliff: ' "Oh, Mr Lockwood, I cannot express what a terrible start I got by the momentary view! Those deep black eyes! That smile, and ghastly paleness! It appeared to me, not Mr Heathcliff, but a goblin" ... "Is he a ghoul or a vampire?" I mused. I had read of such hideous incarnate demons.' This poem confirms the suspicion that *Wuthering Heights* was a natural progression from Gondal, with similar characters and similar settings.

46 their   presumably in error for 'its'.

40 'There was a time when my cheek burned' (October 1839). Another poem, like no. 38, expressing cynicism, misanthropy and rejection of the world's opinion. This combination of attitudes is not something that is natural to the poet, but is rather the result of reaction against earlier years of youthful enthusiasm and idealism. The disillusionment is not total, however: the poet retains her juvenile ideals but is now capable of containing them, being aware that she cannot change the world. Though the poem may reflect Emily's own feelings, in particular her indifference to convention, it more probably belongs in a Gondal context where such emotions were more in keeping.

41 Love and Friendship (undated). This short poem, undated but transcribed into a manuscript book of poetry in February 1844, is on a familiar poetic theme. The rose-briar, with its beautiful flowers and sweet fragrance, is an analogy for love which is exquisite but ephemeral. Contrasted with this is the holly tree which has no showy blossoms but which remains unchanged throughout the year; the holly tree is an analogy for friendship which is not seasonal but constant throughout periods of joy and sorrow alike. There is no indication whether this is a personal or a Gondal poem, though the rejection of love is typical of the embittered heroes of Gondal. Charlotte published the poem in 1850 without alterations, perhaps feeling that it was conventional enough to stand on its own since there was no specific Gondal reference.

Text: 1850.

42 Stanzas to – (14 November 1839). Though the sentiments of this poem have frequently caused commentators to suggest that it refers to Branwell, it is quite clear that it belongs to the world of Gondal. The manuscript dating of the lines and their publication in 1846 – two years before Branwell's death – refute any such suggestion. Nor is there any reason to believe, because of this poem, that Emily was more sympathetic to her brother's plight than the rest of her family, for the lines are clearly written in character. It is easy to see how these Branwell associations have arisen, for the poem is so powerful in both emotion and expression that it is difficult to believe it could not have arisen out of personal experience. The impact of the poem comes from the terseness of the style, which prevents a lapse into sentimentality, and from the sense of immediacy created by the use of direct speech even though the poem is, in effect, a monologue. The last ten lines are particularly memorable and reflect Emily's own passionate love of animals.

Text: 1846.

43 'That wind I used to hear it swelling' (28 November 1839). The wind had particularly rapturous associations for Emily; like the evening hours it had the power of inspiring imagination. In this instance, however, it is not the adventures of an imaginary world that are conjured up, but rather memories of the past. As these memories are so potent that no future delights can outweigh them, it seems unlikely that the poem is a personal one, for Emily was not yet a pessimist; more likely it belongs to the Gondal cycle.

44 Sympathy (undated, but probably November 1839). This short poem was first published by Emily herself in the volume of *Poems* of 1846, under the cryptic title

'Sympathy'. The elegiac mood created by the pictorial images of winter and autumn is sustained by a restrained use of repetition and alliteration: 'They weep . . . you weep' (line 9), 'sigh . . . sighing' (line 10), 'their fate . . . Your fate' (lines 13–14). The poem, nevertheless, is not pessimistic in tone; there is comfort for the mourner not only in the beauties of nature but also in the blessing of memory which cannot be erased. Like the seasons, there is a time for loss and sorrow (the image of winter shedding 'its grief in snow' is a particularly choice one) but the lessons of decline and renewal are also apposite to the human mourner.

Text: 1846.

3 **pours**   sheds (Hatfield MS). For publication in 1846 Emily transposed the verbs in the third and eleventh lines of the manuscript poem, perhaps to avoid the rather clumsy assonance, 'sheds . . . silent . . . sunshine'.
4 **And**   Or (Hatfield MS).
11 **sheds**   pours (Hatfield MS).
13 **these**   they (Hatfield MS).
15 Then, journey onward, not elate (Hatfield MS).
16 **Still**   But (Hatfield MS).

45 **Stanzas** (4 May 1840). This short poem reflects the two main preoccupations of Gondal characters – despair and death. A story obviously lies behind the allusive lines of verse; the dying figure appears to be an abandoned lover, a common motif of both the Gondal and Angrian cycles, while the watcher's own desire for death presupposes some tragedy untold here – perhaps an unrequited love for the dying character. The pessimistic view of the world expressed here is elaborated elsewhere in Emily's poetry and to some extent it explains her withdrawal into the inner world of the imagination. There is a comparison, for instance, between line 2 of this poem and no. 61, lines 7–8: 'So hopeless is the world without/The world within I doubly prize'. The poem was published in 1846 by Emily herself with a couple of alterations from her original manuscript.

Text: 1846.

8 **a**   the (Hatfield MS).
11 **Weary to watch**   I'm sick to see (Hatfield MS).

46 **The Appeal** (18 May 1840). This short but compelling poem was composed only two weeks after no. 45. It has been suggested by Gérin (*Emily Brontë*, p.111) that the appeal 'in which the passion assumes the language of love' is to Emily's so-called 'God of Visions' to asking him restore her mystic visions to her. This is to read too much into the lines, which belong firmly in the world of Gondal and not in Emily's personal experience. The poem is clearly a love poem on a familiar Gondal theme, the abandonment of one of a pair of lovers and their subsequent separation. (It is possible that this deserted lover is identical with the one who is dying in the previous poem). The Gondal setting is confirmed by comparing these lines with the ones written by Anne on 28 August 1840 (no. 72). Not only is the theme identical but also the two poems share the same title, vocabulary and metre, barring a truncated last line in Emily's verses. A further comparison could be made

with *Wuthering Heights* as, for instance, when Heathcliff defied Catherine to haunt him so as not to leave him alone (chapter 16), or when he threw open the windows of the haunted bedchamber at the Heights and begged her ghost to come in (chapter 3).

47 **The Night Wind** (11 September 1840). Unlike many of Emily's poems which plunge straight into their theme with little or no introduction, this poem has an evocative opening which gives it a graphic and immediate setting. The poet, and in this instance she clearly is speaking in her own character, is sitting in the Parsonage parlour late at night while the wind blows through an open window. The wind is here personified and given direct speech so that a conversation between wind and poet is possible. Surprisingly, Emily at first rejects the seductive words of the wind which seeks to draw her back to nature, preferring to leave 'my human feelings in their own course to flow'. As the wind gets ʾe last word it is to be presumed that Emily was won over and abandoned the solitude necessary for her thoughts to accompany the wind in mind at least, if not in physical form. The changes which Charlotte made to the last two verses when she published the poem in 1850 were intended to correct the metre which had suddenly gained an extra syllable in the first and third lines.

25 **leave** heed (1850).
29 Were we not friends from childhood? (1850).
31 As long as thou, the solemn night (1850).
33 **laid at rest** resting (1850).
34 **church-yard** church aisle (1850). A deliberate change on Charlotte's part, for Emily was buried in the family vault beneath Haworth church and not in the churchyard itself.
35 *I* shall have time for mourning (1850).
36 And *thou* for being alone (1850).

48 **The Caged Bird** (27 February 1841). The caged bird is a common motif in literature, serving as a useful metaphor for the human condition. Here the bird is not identified, but knowing Emily's predilection for wild things it is likely that the bird is a hawk. This is consonant with the internal evidence of the poem, for the bird is a frequenter of 'breezy hills' and is confined by a chain rather than a cage as such. In 1841 Emily had her own hawk, rescued from an abandoned nest on the moors. When she returned from Brussels in November 1842 the bird had gone, for she recorded in her diary paper of July 1845 that she had 'lost the hawk Hero, which, with the geese, was given away, and is doubtless dead, for when I came back from Brussels I inquired on all hands and could hear nothing of him' (L. & L., i, 305). Emily's identification with the bird in the poem is total; like it she is alone, longing for liberty and freedom on the moors, but knowing that for both the only release will be the eternal one of death. It is possible that this poem may have a Gondal setting, for a similar image was used by Anne in her poem 'The Captive Dove' (no. 76). Typically, however, Emily longs only for liberty, even if this is attained through death, while Anne is prepared to accept the compromise of a shared captivity as the means of alleviating her lot.

49 'Methinks this heart should rest awhile' (undated). These sixteen lines are usually printed as a continuation of no. 48, even though, as Hatfield pointed out, they are in two separate and distinct manuscripts and have no connection in their subject matter. This short poem is an object lesson to those who try to read autobiography and personal experience into Emily's poetry for, despite its apparently personal context, it is a Gondal poem. Though the evocative description of descending mist could easily refer to Haworth, the initials 'M.A.A.' heading the manuscript and the aristocratic reference to halls (line 4) make it clear that Emily is once more speaking in character. The sad watcher is not Emily, therefore, but rather a fictitious character who foresees in the wintry decline of the flowers which were made for summer sun a premonition of her own death.

50 The Old Stoic (1 March 1841). These twelve lines were first published in the sisters' volume of poetry in 1846, when they were given the title 'The Old Stoic'. Though they are often taken to summarise Emily's philosophy of life, it is more likely that they are spoken through a Gondal character. Despite the attractions of believing Emily to be as liberated from convention as suggested here, the author of Wuthering Heights cannot be said to have laughed love to scorn nor to have had no desire for fame – albeit fame for her work rather than fame for her person. Similarly, in 1841 the twenty-three year old Emily could hardly have believed that her 'swift days' were 'nearing their goal'. Alternatively, there is no doubt that 'liberty was the breath of Emily's nostrils' as Charlotte stated in her preface to the poem, so that the poet identified with the sentiments her character expresses here.

Text: 1846.

11 In   Through (Hatfield MS).
11–12 Compare these lines with no. 69.

51 'Shall Earth no more inspire thee' (16 May 1841). When Charlotte published this poem in 1850 (one of the few she did not heavily edit) she added a helpful note: 'The following little piece has no title, but in it the genius of a solitary region seems to address his wandering and wayward votary, and to recall within his influences the proud mind which rebelled at times against what it most loved.' We have already seen how Emily's 'proud mind' sometimes recoiled from the allurements of nature (no. 47). Here, however, there is no dialogue and Emily's pantheism is seen in its most extreme form, partly because there is no comment from the 'fond idolater' herself. Though a Gondal context is again intimated, the sentiments coincide so exactly with Emily's own, as Charlotte and indeed Emily herself bore witness, that there is little point in trying to separate the two. The ideas introduced in lines 21–4 were further explored in Wuthering Heights where Catherine Earnshaw dreams that she is in heaven: 'heaven did not seem to be my home; and I broke my heart with weeping to come back to earth; and the angels were so angry that they flung me out into the middle of the heath on the top of Wuthering Heights; where I woke sobbing for joy' (chapter 9). Later, in chapter 15, the dying Catherine tells Heathcliff: 'The thing that irks me most is this shattered prison, after all. I'm tired, tired of being enclosed here. I'm wearying to

escape into that glorious world, and to be always there: not seeing it dimly through tears, and yearning for it through the walls of an aching heart; but really with it, and in it.'

Text: 1850

52 'I see around me tombstones grey' (17 July 1841). This poem, written only two months after no. 51, expands on the same theme, though in a darker vein. The opening lines graphically conjure up the view which Emily saw daily from the Parsonage windows. They also set the scene for a poem which concentrates on the human miseries of 'time and death and mortal pain'. These are the sufferings and sorrows to be endured on earth, in stark contrast to the last poem which concentrates solely on the joys of nature. In some ways, therefore, this is the 'fond idolater's' reply to nature's call. The poem contains some startlingly unorthodox ideas which in Emily's lifetime would have condemned her in conventional eyes as unregenerate. The rejection of the Christian heaven which is implicit in many of her poems is here made explicit: 'We would not leave our native home,/For *any* world beyond the tomb' (lines 41–2). In the last lines the poet asks for complete absorption, body and soul, into the earth with no hope of resurrection, or else a life beyond the tomb which is shared with the beloved earth. Here again there is a strong similarity with Catherine's dream of heaven in *Wuthering Heights*, where she wept with joy when she was thrown out of heaven and restored to earth. The poem develops into a Gondal setting and two weeks after it was written Emily recorded in her diary paper that she had a good many books on hand, 'but I am sorry to say that as usual I make slow progress with any' (L. & L., i, 216).

53 How Clear She Shines! (13 April 1843). This poem, written nearly six months after Emily's return from Brussels, shows remarkably little change or progression in her thoughts since her departure. Indeed, the nine months in Brussels, despite their surely momentous effect on a girl who had only left home three times before for short intervals at local schools, left little or no trace on Emily's development, unlike Charlotte for whom it was a formative experience. This poem returns to the old familiar themes, contrasting the real world with which Emily had little sympathy and the imaginary world in which she found her excitement and her satisfaction. The real world, with its corruption and false views, is temporarily to be forgotten while the dreamer seeks solace in the powers of imagination which, as always, are stimulated by the hours of night. The hope remains that there is another world beyond the real one where virtue will be prized and where death will not rule with despotic sway. The poem was published with a few alterations by Emily herself in 1846.

Text: 1846.

2 **guardian** silver (Hatfield MS).
10 **conceal** go hide (Hatfield MS).
36 **surest** shortest (Hatfield MS).

54 'Yes, holy be thy resting place' (undated, but poems on other side of leaf dated

26 July 1843). A poem from the Gondal cycle which probably represents Augusta Geraldine Almeda's farewell to her wronged husband, Lord Alfred of Aspin Castle. At the command of her lover, Julius Brenzaida, she has sent Lord Alfred away so that she can live with Julius as her husband, but she is afflicted by pangs of conscience, which Lord Alfred's later suicide, in exile, for love of her do nothing to alleviate. In this poem Augusta bids Lord Alfred an affectionate farewell and expresses the hope that the Fates will be kind to him and wishes him well for the future. The piquancy of the poem lies in the fact that it is put in the mouth of Augusta, who is in the most complex moral situation, loving Julius passionately, but still caring for Lord Alfred. The mention of the 'resting-place' in the first two lines is prophetic in that, as a suicide, Lord Alfred's spirit is unable to find rest and returns to wander round his ancestral halls at Aspin Castle. Lines 21–4 echo the beginning of another poem dated 2 March 1844 which is headed 'A[ugusta] G[eraldine] A[lmeda] to A[lfred] S.':

> This summer wind with thee and me
> Roams in the dawn of day;
> But thou must be where it shall be,
> Ere Evening – far away. (Hatfield, p.197)

55 **Warning and Reply** (6 September 1843). A Gondal poem, published by Charlotte in 1850 under the title 'Warning and Reply'. The poem takes the form of a soliloquy, part of which is expressed in direct speech. The poet is reminded of her mortality; death will come one day and cut her off from everything and everyone she has loved and confine her to the tomb. To this the poet replies that she welcomes death for the rest it brings: she has nothing to fear from separation for none of her friends are true to her on earth. There is only one heart on earth that will lament her, though that heart is a worthy one. The identity of the narrator, called 'E.' at the head of the manuscript, is not clear, though Ratchford identifies 'E.' as a relative of Gerald, a prince of Gondal deposed by Julius Brenzaida. The changes which Charlotte made to the poem when she published it in 1850 were dictated by her desire to correct Emily's lapses in metre.

8 twinèd   entwined (1850).
12 its gloom and thee   it shudderingly (1850).
15 they'll   they will (1850).
23 broke only there   breaks only – here (1850).
24 That [italic]: But that (1850).

56 **Castle Wood** (2 February 1844). A typical Gondal poem on the familiar theme of the fated being, who has been made cynical through disillusionment with life – and who now faces death with equanimity because he has no ties on earth. Ratchford has suggested that this character is Amadeus, the 'dark boy of sorrow', who to some extent prefigures Heathcliff; she believes that this poem is Amadeus' comment on the fact that he has been chosen by lot to assassinate the Gondal emperor, Julius Brenzaida, knowing all the while that he was likely to be killed in

the attempt (as indeed happened). However, the initials A.S. at the top left-hand corner of the manuscript indicate that the character may be Alfred, lord of Aspin Castle, who died by his own hand in England where he had been exiled by Augusta Geraldine Almeda after her love affair with him had begun to bore her. The deeply pessimistic tones of this poem and Alfred's own hopelessly unrequited love for Augusta would also make these lines apposite for his final speech before committing suicide. This fearless attitude in the face of death, which also occurs in other poems, arises not from faith or hope in a world to come, but rather from estrangement and disillusionment with the present world.

57 'Fall, leaves, fall' (undated). A fragment, probably the beginning of a longer poem which did not develop from these opening lines. The hauntingly musical quality of the lines is emphasised by the melancholic atmosphere of autumn closing into winter. This contrasts with the poet's feelings which, contrary to convention, look forward to winter rather than spring. There is a happy choice of phrase at lines 5–6, where the theme of seasonal flowers and leaves is carried over into the 'wreaths of snow' which blossom just like the rose they replace.

58 'All day I've toiled' (undated but preceded in the manuscript by a poem dated 27 July 1839). An unusually tranquil poem which could be personal in that it is set in Emily's favourite evening hour and she is known to have pursued erratic studies in her own free time; it is more likely however that it belongs to the Gondal cycle. Ratchford suggests that the narrator is Julius Brenzaida, who in his youthful days at the Palace of Instruction in Gaaldine had been the best scholar there, but is rapidly in danger of being eclipsed by Rosina of Alcona (probably an alias for Augusta Geraldine Almeda). Jealous of the fact that Julius alone has withheld his approval of her talents, Rosina/Augusta sets out to seduce him, so that this poem represents the last halcyon days before he is plunged into her world of deceit and power-games. Though the poem would thus belong very early in the Gondal cycle, Emily and Anne frequently rewrote their favourite passages and returned to the earlier stories to elaborate upon them with the benefit of hindsight.

59 The Wanderer from the Fold (11 March 1844). Clement Shorter suggested that this poem, lamenting the way that the subject went astray in life, was 'probably the last poem composed by Emily Brontë and refers, doubtless, to her brother, Patrick Branwell Brontë . . .' Neither of these surmises was correct, though Charlotte's pencilled heading in the manuscript, 'On a life perverted', and the title she gave it when she published it in 1850, 'The Wanderer from the Fold', suggest that she may have seen a parallel between the lives of the subject and her brother. However, the manuscript is dated 11 March 1844 – a period when Branwell was apparently doing well as a tutor at Thorp Green – and is headed 'E.W. to A.G.A.'. These are clearly Gondal characters; A.G.A. is Augusta Geraldine Almeda, Queen of Gondal, and E.W. is Lord Eldred W., Captain of the Queen's Guard, who was her lifelong friend and faithful retainer. Lord Eldred frequently appears as the narrator or bystander who observes the chaotic events of the kingdoms with both objectivity and sensitivity. Here he appears in his usual

role, mourning the death of Augusta who has been murdered at her stepdaughter's instigation and who is forgotten by everyone but himself, despite her passionate friendships and loves. Here he laments the quirk of fortune which turned the beautiful and brilliant child into a heartless, pleasure-loving and power-seeking Queen.

14 Love and Gladness   sinless sunshine (1850).
15 Memory   presence (1850).
16 Like gladsome summer day (1850).
20 That   Which (1850).
31 that   which (1850).

60 Song (1 May 1844). This most evocative of laments is, like no. 59, pronounced over the grave of Augusta Geraldine Almeda, the murdered Queen of Gondal, by her faithful Captain of Guards, Lord Eldred W., whose initials appear at the bottom of the manuscript. As an elegy it is outstanding for the beauty and simplicity of its language and the genuine sorrow of the mourner which is implicit, though never explicitly stated. The contrast between Eldred's deep emotion and the shallow outburst of grief among Augusta's former lovers is effectively drawn. The most powerful image is that of the quiet, untroubled grave contrasted with her frenetic lifestyle which brought grief and despair to so many. It is an image which is repeated to similar effect as the closing lines of *Wuthering Heights*, where Mr Lockwood visits the graves of Catherine, Heathcliff and Edgar Linton: 'I lingered round them, under the benign sky; watched the moths fluttering among the heath and harebells, listened to the soft wind breathing through the grass, and wondered how any one could ever imagine unquiet slumbers for the sleepers in that quiet earth' (chapter 34). The poem was selected by Emily for publication in 1846, and she made no alterations to the manuscript text, suggesting that it already met with her approval.
    Text: 1846.

61 To Imagination (3 September 1844). This hymn to the powers of the mind was published by Emily herself in 1846, and given the title 'To Imagination'. In many ways it summarises the central importance of imagination to Emily Brontë's life. For her it was an escape from the drudgery of her ordinary life, a solace from all the sorrows and ills of the real world and an inspiration for the future. In this poem, though imagination is personified, it does not have the separate will and separate identity which it appears to have in other poems (see, for example, no. 67); indeed, here it almost seems to be subject to herself, for in her inner world 'thou, and I, and Liberty,/Have undisputed sovereignty.' Though she relies on the power of the imagination to bring her comfort and hope, the poet is not dependent on it, nor yet deluded by it into believing that it provides the answer to the problems of the real world. Emily's contempt for and rejection of society and conventional values are expressed at their pithiest in lines 7–8. Though the poem may have originated in a Gondal context, Emily's own poetic outpourings reveal only too clearly her absorption in the world of imagination.
    Text: 1846.

14 **guilt**   grief (Hatfield MS).
16 **untroubled**   unsullied (Hatfield MS).
26 **vision**   visions (Hatfield MS).
36 **sweeter**   brighter (Hatfield MS).

62 **Plead for Me** (14 October 1844). This poem, published in 1846, has close affinities with no. 61 which was written less than six weeks earlier. Again the subject is imagination, but this time, instead of praising its powers and the solace it brings, the poet rebels against its sway. She questions what has made her choose the path of imagination which has led her so far out of the common walks of men. The curiously ambivalent relationship between the poet and this 'God of Visions', which was hinted at in no. 61, is explained at length in this poem. Imagination is personified as a being with a separate entity who is at one and the same time slave, comrade and king of the poet; slave because it is subject to her will, comrade because it is always present, and king because it has her under its sway. The demand in the last line, 'And tell why I have chosen thee!', thus becomes rhetorical since the poet has already given the answer herself.

Text: 1846.

1 **Oh, thy**   O thy (Hatfield MS).
20 **mine** [italic]   mine (Hatfield MS).
33 **earthly**   real (Hatfield MS).

63 **The Philosopher** (3 February 1845). Whether or not this poem has a personal or a Gondal context, the powerful imagery suggests a passionate identification with the 'space-sweeping soul' of the philosopher. Once again, Emily uses dialogue to great effect to create a sense of immediacy and there are echoes of former themes here. The rejection of the conventional Christian heaven (and hell) in favour of the dreamless sleep of death is prefigured, for instance, in no. 52, but the reasoning behind the rejection is different. This time it is simply to end the internal conflict of heart, soul and mind which are tearing apart the human frame within which they are confined. The philosopher only seeks oblivion, however, because he has failed to find the life-giving spirit which would enable the three warring factions to be channelled into a single revelatory power of unparalleled dimensions. The apocalyptic vision of the spirit creating not only order but also power out of the chaos caused by the disparate trends is not to be realised, therefore, and the only acceptable alternative is 'senseless rest'. This view of death as the end of all things contrasts sharply with Emily's views expressed elsewhere (see nos. 48 and 50) that death is equated wth liberty, releasing the soul from the chains of the flesh in order to achieve a sort of mystic union with the freedom of eternity. This poem was singled out by the critic of the *Athenaeum* in July 1846 for particular praise and lengthy quotation as an example of Emily's 'power of wing' as a poet. (Gérin, *Emily Brontë*, pp.194–5.)

Text: 1846.

35 **sent**   bent (Hatfield MS).

36 through   on (Hatfield MS).

40 its   the (Hatfield MS).

51 senseless   lifeless (Hatfield MS). A change made to emphasise the contrast between 'senseless' rest and 'sentient' soul.

55 And vanquished Good, victorious Ill (Hatfield MS).

64 Remembrance (3 March 1845). A poem from the Gondal cycle entitled 'R[osina] Alcona to J[ulius] Brenzaida' which was published in 1846 by Emily under the title 'Remembrance', though at least one significant change was made to obscure its Gondal origins. The poem is a lament by Rosina Alcona (which appears to be a pseudonym for Augusta Geraldine Almeda), for Julius Brenzaida, the emperor of Gondal who had been assassinated fifteen years before. Despite Augusta's many lovers and her casually cruel attitude towards them, Julius had been the one great and true love of her life, whose memory time could not efface. This poem perhaps best illustrates what Charlotte called the 'peculiar music – wild, melancholy and elevating' which so impressed her on first reading Emily's poetry. The musical resonance of the poem is emphasised by the repetition of key words and phrases and a liberal use of alliteration.

Text: 1846.

4 all-severing   all wearing (Hatfield MS).

6 that northern shore   Angora's shore (Hatfield MS). Angora was one of the four provinces of Gondal; this reference to Gondal was removed when the poem was published in 1846.

8 Thy   That (Hatfield MS).

15 Other . . . other   Sterner . . . darker (Hatfield MS).

17 later light   other sun (Hatfield MS).

18 second morn   other Star (Hatfield MS).

65 Death (10 April 1845). Another lament, written only a month after no. 64, but viewing death with the bitterness of recent loss rather than with the softening effect of memory tinged with melancholy. The poem is also much less personal because the mourner's life is seen in terms of metaphor: she is a branch upon the tree of time, flourishing in the spring of youth, dying back in the autumn and winter of sinful maturer age but blossoming even brighter in the second May which is equated with the love which 'had power to keep it from all wrong'. However, at this very moment of fulfilment, death removed the loved one, leaving the mourner's life blighted and hopeless. The mourner therefore appeals for death too, so that, continuing the metaphor, her 'withered branch' will be lopped off the tree of life but the 'mouldering corpse' will continue the cycle of life by nourishing 'That from which it sprung – Eternity'. The elaborate metaphor, ending as the mourner desired to do, where it began, is one of Emily's most complex. The poem is clearly a Gondal one, possibly relating to Julius Brenzaida's murder, but it is treated in a more philosophical manner than her earlier poems, reflecting the maturity of her later style.

Text: 1846.

20 **that**   its (Hatfield MS).
25 **Cruel**   Heartless (Hatfield MS).

66 The Visionary (9 Ocrober 1845). This is the opening of a much longer poem from the Gondal cycle entitled 'Julian M. and A.G. Rochelle'. The first twelve lines were published in 1850 by Charlotte who added a further eight lines of her own to make it stand as a complete poem in its own right. She did this because Emily had already published lines 13–44 in the 1846 volume of poems (see no. 67). The whole poem, without Charlotte's interpolations or Emily's omissions is printed in Hatfield pp.236–41. The two shorter extracts here (nos. 66 and 67) include the best lines and have an interest of their own in that they are the lines the sisters wanted the world to see.

The poem as Emily wrote it, relates the earthly loves of two Gondal figures of noble rank, one of whom, Julian, is the defiant watcher in the house, waiting for A.G. Rochelle's secret visit. The reason for the secrecy is not fully explained though the lovers are in the Romeo and Juliet situation of coming from warring families and, as the full poem reveals, Julian had fallen in love with and released Rochelle from his kinsmen's prison. Charlotte's interpolations completely change the poem here, however, for instead of reverting to the memory of their first meeting in prison it ends with the watcher welcoming a spiritual visitation, a messenger of hope. The watcher has thus become Emily herself, and not her Gondal character, making nonsense of the guiding light in the window, but making it in keeping with many of Emily's own compositions where Imagination is personified as an external, physical presence.

Text: 1850.

4 **drift**   drifts (Hatfield MS).
12 **frozen**   winter (Hatfield MS).
13–20 These lines were written and interpolated by Charlotte.

67 The Prisoner: a fragment (9 October 1845). This poem was first published by Emily in 1846, when it was given the title 'The Prisoner: a fragment'; like no. 66 (see above), it is derived from the long Gondal poem entitled 'Julian M. to A.G. Rochelle', the first 60 lines of 'The Prisoner' being lines 13–44 and 65–92 of the original Gondal piece; the last stanza was added by Emily for publication in 1846. The sections of the Gondal composition not published by Emily in 1846 or Charlotte in 1850 were the narrative ones, which could not be published without laying the world of Gondal before an uncomprehending public. The poem contains one of the most quoted passages of Emily's poetry which describes in lyric terms a mystic experience of overwhelming power. Though the context is clearly Gondal the immediacy of the language and the graphic descriptions of the physical effect of the withdrawal of the 'divine vision' have led most commentators to believe that the character is merely a mouthpiece for Emily's personal experience. The visitant is equated with the 'Benignant Power' of no. 61 and the 'God of Visions' of no. 62, and Emily's visionary powers are compared to those of St Theresa of Avila and St John of the Cross. Their Christian experience, however, is essentially different from Emily's personification and worship of the imagination as a quasi-independent power, even though her language does, on occasion, assume religious overtones.

Text: 1846.

28 that   which (Hatfield MS).
31 kindred's   parents' (Hatfield MS).
32 In the full original manuscript, 20 lines omitted here are included. They explain how Julian and A.G. Rochelle recognised each other as childhood friends and Julian is moved to pity by the beauty of his captive.
33 'Still, let my tyrants know,': Yet, tell them Julian, all (Hatfield MS).
61 turned to go   watched here there (Hatfield MS).
62–4 Not daring now to touch one lock of silken hair
    As I had knelt in scorn, on the dank floor I knelt still
    My fingers in the links of that iron hard and chill. (Hatfield MS.)
64 In the full version of the poem 56 lines omitted here tell how Julian falls in love with and secretly releases his beautiful captive; for thirteen weeks he hides and nurses her until she finally repays his devotion by returning his love.

68 Stanzas (manuscript lost). These twenty lines, which are among Emily's best, have aroused considerable controversy over their authorship since they seem to give an outsider's view of Emily rather than her own personal view. Hatfield (pp.255–6) thought they were by Charlotte; Willett (BST: 18:92: 143–8) suggested Anne. As Chitham has pointed out, however (BST: 18:93: 222–6), though Charlotte sometimes corrected metrical inconsistencies and obfuscated Gondal references when editing her sister's poetry, she did not stoop to fraud and would not have passed these lines off as Emily's if she had written them herself. Likewise, the last stanza is far too pantheistic for the deeply religious Anne to have written. There is therefore no reason to doubt Emily's authorship; indeed, the poem seems typical of her work, exploring ideas which recur in other poems. As the one member of the family who did not repeatedly try to earn her own living she may well have felt 'Often rebuked' by her own conscience, particularly as this left her time to indulge in imagination. Having abandoned all hope of a career for the world of imagination, for once she also rejects Gondal since it threatens to engulf her, though the emphatic placing of 'Today' at the beginning of line 5 makes it clear this is only a temporary repudiation. The worlds of intellect and imagination, on this occasion, are to be subjugated to the sensual pleasure of feeling and it is the moors, which, being so akin to Emily's own nature, have the power to awaken her emotions.

Text: 1850.

3–4 Compare with no. 62, lines 11–15.
5 the shadowy region   i.e. Gondal.

69 No Coward Soul Is Mine (25 January 1846, misdated to 2 January 1846 by

Hatfield). This magnificent poem was first published after Emily's death by Charlotte, who noted that 'the following are the last lines my sister Emily ever wrote'. This was not true, for in the three-year interval before she died Emily wrote several more extant poems, her novel *Wuthering Heights* and probably began a second novel. There may have been other poems too which have not survived. Given the fact that these lines are unique among Emily's poems because of their religious theme, it is not surprising that Charlotte would have wanted to believe that this great statement of personal faith should be her sister's last poetic effort. Typically, the God that Emily worships is not the human Christ of Anne's poetry, but rather the omnipotent, omni-present God, the source of life. He is not bounded within the different creeds but is spiritually and physically both a part of and external to her own being – much the same sort of dual existence that imagination had enjoyed in earlier poems. Emily's contempt for sectarian religion is nowhere expressed more strongly than here, though the caricature of Jabes Branderham in *Wuthering Heights* also made her feelings plain. Characteristically, and contrasting with the ephemeral nature of most forms of worship, it is the eternity of God that is the central theme of this poem.

14 thy thine (1850).
21 moon man (1850). A misreading of the manuscript by Charlotte.
23 wert were (1850).
27 Since thou Thou – THOU (1850).
28 thou THOU (1850).

70 The North Wind (26 January 1838). This poem is written in the character of Alexandrina Zenobia, one of the heroines of the Gondal stories, who was frequently used by Anne as the narrator of her poems. Alexandrina suffers the usual Gondal fates of exile, separation from her childhood sweetheart and imprisonment. This poem, addressed to the north wind, purports to be written from prison; the wind is personified and given a voice with which it creates a powerful evocation of the beloved homeland of the prisoner. Its song reduces her to tears but the pain of recalling freedom and the mountains of home is preferable to the numbing misery of hopeless despair. This poem is a companion to one written by Emily the previous month addressed to a wreath of snow (Hatfield, pp.57–8). Anne's poem was apparently written while she was convalescing from a serious illness which she had contracted while a pupil at Miss Wooler's school (L. & L., i, 145).

71 The Bluebell (22 August 1840). In the spring of 1840 Anne left Haworth to take up a post as governess to the Robinson family at Thorp Green near York, where she was to remain for five years. The poem is clearly both personal and autobiographical; the setting and the fact that she felt 'less harassed than at other times' suggest that it was written during the Robinsons' annual August holiday at Scarborough. The temporary alleviation of her duties has caused an unusual buoyancy of spirits which the sight of the bluebell, reminding her of her home and happy childhood, immediately dispels. The contrast between her past and present life is a bitter one. Anne expanded her views on the drudgery of the life of a governess in her novel *Agnes Grey* where a similar incident occurs. Agnes, walking home from church, feels her usual spirit of misanthropy evaporating away in the sunshine: 'I longed intensely for some familiar flower that might recall the woody dales or green hill-sides of home: the brown moor-lands, of course, were out of the question. Such a discovery would make my eyes gush out with water, no doubt; but that was one of my greatest enjoyments now' (chapter 13). Emily shared Anne's sentiments about the bluebell, which both sisters appear to have confused with the harebell, and wrote a similar poem where it inspires recollections of home (see no. 37 and notes).

72 **Appeal** (28 August 1840). The manuscript title, 'Lines Written at Thorp Green', suggests that this poem is a personal one reflecting the homesickness that bedevilled Anne's attempts to earn a living. When Anne published it in the 1846 volume of *Poems* she changed the title to 'Appeal', obviously to preserve the anonymity of 'Acton Bell'. It is more likely, however, that this apparently heartfelt plea, with its spare but eloquent use of words, belongs to the Gondal cycle. As Ratchford pointed out, Emily wrote a very similar poem, also entitled 'The Appeal' (no. 46); her poem, written in the May before Anne's, employs a similarly economical style and also combines expressions of grief and loneliness with a plea for a lover to return. Since the separation of lovers was a constantly reiterated theme in Gondal poetry, it is more probable that the poem belongs to the fantasy world than to Anne's personal experience.

Text: 1846.

73 **Lines Written at Thorp Green** (19 August 1841). Another auto-biographical poem arising from Anne's sense of loneliness and isolation as a governess at Thorp Green. Anne was evidently very unhappy at this period. In the diary papers which she and Emily wrote on 30 July 1841, Emily ended hers by 'sending from far an exhortation of courage, boys! courage, to exiled and harassed Anne, wishing she was here' (L. & L., i, 216). Anne herself wrote, 'I am governess in the family of Mr Robinson. I dislike the situation and wish to change it for another . . . I have the same faults that I had then [1837, when the last diary paper was written], only I have more wisdom and experience, and a little more self-possession than I then enjoyed' (L. & L., i, 217). Only twelve days before this poem was written, Charlotte added a postscript to her letter to Ellen Nussey about Anne: 'She has so much to endure: far, far more than I have . . . [I] always see her as a patient, persecuted stranger . . . She is more lonely, less gifted with the power of making friends, even than I am' (L. & L., i, 219).

5–6 There were four months to go before Anne's next holiday at home.
14 The bluebell was one of Anne's favourite flowers, see no. 71.
23 The long winter evenings at Haworth were especially precious to the Brontë sisters, for this was the time they devoted to writing.

74 **Despondency** (20 December 1841). This poem, written during the Christmas

holidays of 1841, reveals the deeply religious side of Anne. It is perhaps surprising that such a gloomy poem should have been written when she was at her happiest reunited with the family at home. However, it seems likely that she was troubled about whether or not to return to Thorp Green: on 10 January 1842 Charlotte told Ellen Nussey. 'Anne has rendered herself so valuable in her difficult situation that they have entreated her to return to them, if it be but for a short time. I almost think she will go back, if we can get a good servant who will do all our work' (L. & L., i, 226). The decision was complicated by the fact that Charlotte and Emily were about to go to Brussels, leaving Mr Brontë on his own. Anne must have felt rather left out of their plans and torn as to whether to remain at home and look after their father or return to Thorp Green to earn her own living so as to reduce the financial burden caused by the Brussels scheme. Possibly as a result of Aunt Branwell's early religious instruction Anne had a deep sense of personal sin and doubts as to her salvation; like all the Brontës, however, she firmly rejected the Calvinist view of predestination and eternal damnation, believing instead in universal salvation.

36 Charlotte watered this line down to 'Christ, hear my humble prayer' (1850). Anne's choice of the more expressive 'wretch' was probably influenced by evangelical usage.

75 **Lines Composed in a Wood on a Windy Day** (30 December 1842). Anne's note, written on the manuscript of this poem, 'Composed in the Long Plantation on a wild, bright, windy day', suggests that this poem arose from actual experience. The unusual and insistent metre is used to great effect to simulate the gusting force of the wind; Emily had used a similar metre with a dactylic rhythm, in her earlier poem 'High waving heather' (no. 27) as a device to recreate an atmosphere of storm and flood. Although we have no description of Anne's first visit to the sea, as we have of Charlotte's, in her 1841 diary paper she recorded that in the last four years 'I have been a governess at Blake Hall, left it, come to Thorp Green, and seen the sea and York Minster' (L. & L., i, 217). Like Charlotte, Anne was profoundly moved by the sea as her description in lines 9–12 suggests, and it is no coincidence that she chose to spend her last days on the Yorkshire coast at Scarborough.

76 **The Captive Dove** (31 October 1843). Anne's note on the manuscript states that this poem was 'Mostly written in the spring of 1842'. The image of the caged bird is a common one in literature and the concomitant themes of confinement and loss of liberty are recurrent in Gondal poetry. Emily wrote a poem on the same subject (no. 48), but her treatment was totally different from Anne's, even though each sister identified strongly with her particular bird. For Emily the important element was the deprivation of liberty, 'Give we the hills our equal prayer': her consolation lies in the thought that death will restore liberty to both captives. For Anne the imprisonment, though unnatural, is an accepted destiny from which there is no escape, but which a sympathetic companionship could make not merely tolerable but even pleasurable. Though it is probable that both poems are meant to be read in a Gondal context, it is difficult to escape the

conclusion that they reflect the authors' attitude to life. For Emily, the confinement of the schoolroom at Roe Head and later at Law Hill was spiritually and physically unendurable and was of short duration. For Anne, the loneliness of an uncongenial occupation as governess was a duty which must be borne regardless of personal preference.

77 The Consolation (7 November 1843). This appears to be a personal poem, despite the fact that a Gondal setting is indicated by the signature 'Hespera Caverndel', an unidentifiable figure from the imaginary world. At the very least, Anne is here writing in a character whose situation is similar to her own. The opening lines depict an autumnal setting consonant with the November date of the poem. The poet's melancholy is not purely seasonal, however, but deepened by her sense of isolation from the rest of her family and her longing for the sympathetic companionship of home. The poem was first published by Anne herself in 1846.
  Text: 1846.

14 & 16 youthful joys . . . noon of day   Anne was only twenty-three when she
  wrote this poem, despite her cynical view.

78 Past Days (21 November 1843). This wistful poem was the third that Anne wrote in three weeks on the same theme, her loneliness and her longing for the comradeship of home (see nos. 76 and 77). Its effectiveness lies in the contrast implicit between the simple happiness of the past which the poem describes and the unspoken misery of the present. The contrast is deepened by the use of the negative, particularly in the first and last verses, to highlight the differences between 'then' and 'now'. Anne published the poem in 1846, giving it then the title 'Past Days'.
  Text: 1846.

79 A Reminiscence (April 1844). This poem, first published in 1846, when it was given the title 'A Reminiscence', is usually taken to refer to the Reverend William Weightman, Mr Brontë's curate from August 1839 until his tragically early death at the age of twenty-eight in 1842. All the Brontë family seem to have had a soft spot for him: in the funeral sermon he preached for his curate Mr Brontë said: 'His character wore well; the surest proof of real worth. He had, it is true, some peculiar advantages. Agreeable in person and manners, and constitutionally cheerful, his first introduction was prepossessing. But what he gained at first, he did not lose afterwards. He had those qualities which enabled him rather to gain ground.'

  A bright spark who was immediately admitted into the family circle, Weightman was a steadying influence on Branwell and, according to Ellen Nussey, Emily's only exception among the curates for any conventional courtesy. Charlotte seems to have had a mild flirtation with him, but during the Christmas holidays of 1841 Mr Weightman appears to have turned his attentions to Anne who was home from her post at Thorp Green. Charlotte told Ellen Nussey: 'He sits opposite to Anne at Church sighing softly and looking out of the corners of his eyes to win her attention – and Anne is so quiet, her look so downcast – they are a picture' (Gérin, *Charlotte Brontë*, p.179). This passage is the basis of the story of the love affair between Anne and Mr Weightman, to which the evidence of several poems, including this one, has been added. Though Anne clearly held him in great affection, as indeed did the rest of her family, there is nothing to suggest that her feelings were any deeper. This poem, written eighteen months after Weightman's death, should be taken at face value: it was natural that Anne should lament the loss of the light, kind heart that 'gladdened once our humble sphere', but this poem is by no means an elegy on the death of a lover. Indeed, the general tone of the poem is not tragic, but almost hymn-like in its thankfulness for the life of Weightman.

Text: 1846.

4 Weightman was buried in the vaults beneath Haworth Church.

8 Weightman was renowned for his abundant kindnesses, ranging from walking ten miles to post valentines to the Brontë girls (see no. 10) to his quiet charities in the village.

14 Charlotte referred to Mr Weightman as 'our bonny faced friend', mentioning his 'blue eyes, auburn hair, and rosy cheeks' (L. & L., i, 204, 206): he was evidently good-looking – and knew himself to be so.

80 **Music on Christmas Morning** (manuscript lost, but first published in 1846). This poem was probably written during Anne's time as governess at Thorp Green, but as she always spent the Christmas holidays at home, it was most likely written at Haworth. The bells she heard, however, cannot have been those of Haworth Church, for the peal of six bells paid for by public subscription and cast in 1845 were rung for the first time on 10 March 1846 – only two months before the poem's publication in the sisters' volume of poetry. Many of the phrases of this poem are strongly reminiscent of lines from hymns and carols and the whole composition takes the form of a hymn. As a personal statement of faith by Anne, it is one of her most quietly confident, looking rather to Christ's redeeming powers than to her own sin. The last two verses are particularly interesting in that they underline Anne's (unusual) belief in universal salvation; for her, Christ was a redeemer capable of saving all men after a period of punishment for sins committed, and no sinner, however blackly dyed, was eternally damned.

Text: 1846.

81 **Night** (early 1845). This little poem, which is imprecisely dated on the manuscript, probably has a Gondal setting. It echoes the sentiments and, indeed, the phraseology of certain poems by Emily. For Emily, evening was the part of the day most conducive to poetic inspiration, heralding the play of imagination and dreams. Similarly, 'exiled and harassed Anne', worn down by the continual demands of her employment, found refuge in dreams at nightfall – the only time she could expect some privacy. Though it has been suggested that it is Weightman she recalls in her dreams, this seems unlikely; the dream figure is long dead (lines 6, 9) whereas Weightman had been dead for only just two years; line 9, 'Cold in

the grave for years has lain', clearly echoes Emily's line, 'Cold in the earth, and fifteen wild Decembers' (no. 64) from a poem which undoubtedly has a Gondal setting and which was written in March 1845 – about the same time as this poem by Anne; the term 'the darling of my heart' (line 12) is far stronger than any other employed by Anne with reference to Weightman. Given these factors, it seems most likely that Anne is speaking through a Gondal character, though perhaps the immediate inspiration came from Anne's own dreams at nightfall.

82 Home (manuscript lost, but first published in 1846). Anne's homesickness was one of her most fruitful sources of poetic inspiration. Here we have another poem on the subject, though this time from a slightly different angle. Previous poems contrasted her isolation as a governess among uncongenial and unsympathetic people with the spiritual warmth and comfort of home. This poem, though concluding with a similar refrain, compares her physical surroundings with those of home. The soft, undulating, heavily wooded landscape of the plain of York stands in stark contrast to the barren hills of Haworth where trees are 'scattered and stunted' by the strength of the wind. Similarly, the rich, carefully tended formal gardens of Thorp Green are compared unfavourably to the small neglected garden of Haworth Parsonage. Though the physical surroundings at Thorp Green were therefore far more conventionally attractive than those of Haworth, their actual attractiveness was in inverse proportion to their beauty. There are a number of strong similarities with Emily's poem 'A little while' (no. 36), written as early as December 1838, so Anne may have been influenced by the earlier poem.

Text: 1846.

11–12 Compare with Emily, no. 36, lines 9–10.
21 Compare with Emily, no. 36, line 9.
23–4 Compare with Emily, no. 36, lines 18–19.

83 If This Be All (20 May 1845). Anne seems to have been at her lowest ebb when she wrote this poem. It plumbs the very depths of misery and, unusually for Anne, is completely lacking in hope: the only prospect for an end to her unbearable load is that of death. The dating of the poem is particularly significant, for it was written possibly only days before Anne's leaving Thorp Green 'of her own accord', according to Emily (L. & L., i, 304). By 18 June she was home and still in a depressed state of mind, recording in her diary paper of 31 July 1845 that she could not be 'flatter and older in mind than I am now' (L. & L., i, 307). The reason behind her misery and, indeed, her leaving Thorp Green, was Branwell's conduct. Since January 1843 he had been tutor to the Robinson boy and one month after Anne's resignation he was dismissed from his post. He arrived home in a shattered state, mentally and physically, declaring that a clandestine affair with Mrs Robinson had caused his dismissal. The truth of his story has been doubted, but the Brontë household clearly believed his version of events. Anne's unexpected resignation lends credence to the story and suggests that she had become aware of the affair and took the only course available to extricate herself from an increasingly difficult situation. This poem, written just before the storm broke, reflects Anne's heavy burden of cares which necessarily at that ime she had to bear alone.

Text: 1846.

9 The loss of friendship has sometimes been taken to be that of Emily, since their earlier close collaboration had been interrupted by Anne's continuing employment away from home. It is more likely to be that of Branwell to whose company Anne must have looked forward but whose absorption with his own affairs left little time for his sister.

13–16 Compare with nos. 73, 77 and 78.

17 The Brontës all considered Mrs Robinson to be the seducer and Branwell her unwitting victim.

21–4 Did Anne perhaps offer advice to her brother which was rejected?

29–33 Anne took neither of these options, preferring to resign altogether from her intolerable situation.

84 'Oh, they have robbed me of the hope' (manuscript lost, but first published 1847). Poetry and prose were always intermixed in the Brontës' juvenile writings, the poems acting as focal points for the emotions. In Agnes Grey this poem serves the same function. Agnes has been prevented from seeing or meeting the curate, Mr Weston, whom she has secretly grown to love, by the malicious intervention of her pupils. In her unhappiness, Agnes turns to writing poetry: 'lest the reader should be curious to see any of these effusions, I will favour him with one short specimen: cold and languid as the lines may seem, it was almost a passion of grief to which they owed their being'. After the poem Agnes comments: 'Yes, at least, they could not deprive me of that: I could think of him day and night; and I could feel that he was worthy to be thought of. Nobody knew him as I did; nobody could love him as I – could, if I might' (chapter 17).

This poem is clearly written in the character of Agnes Grey, just as other poems were written in the character of Gondal figures, and there is no evidence whatsoever to suggest that it was originally written about William Weightman, who shared none of Mr Weston's physical or spiritual characteristics, except kindness of heart and unobtrusive charity to the poor.

85 'Farewell to thee' (manuscript lost, but first published 1848). This poem, like no. 84, belongs in the midst of one of Anne's prose compositions, this time her novel The Tenant of Wildfell Hall. Again it forms a focal point for the emotions but this time it is not of the heroine's writing. The poem is a ballad sung by Annabella Wilmot to Lord Lowborough, but in the presence of Helen Graham and the man she loves, Arthur Huntingdon. 'The air was simple, sweet, and sad, it is still running in my head, – and so are the words' (chapter 19). The music and sentiments of the song so nearly coincided with Helen's own feelings about Huntingdon that they reduced her to tears, so that she had to flee the company. Her emotion did not pass unnoticed, however, and Huntingdon followed her and took advantage of her weakness to propose marriage to her. Her acceptance and the consequences of the unlucky match are the subject of the novel. The poem is

therefore central to the story. Ironically, Annabella, now married to Lowborough, becomes Huntingdon's mistress and it is the corrupting influence of the adulterers which drives Helen to take her infant son and leave Huntingdon.

86 The Narrow Way (24 April 1848). This poem, which has become one of Anne's most popular contributions to the hymn book, is a confident assertion of faith expressed in the simple yet ardent phraseology typical of the evangelist movement. The images employed are strongly reminiscent of those in John Bunyan's *Pilgrim's Progress*, one of the favourite books of the Brontë family. The man seeking to enter heaven has an upward path to tread: he is beset on all sides by the lures of sin and, as a soldier of Christ, he has to fight a constant battle against evil. Inspired by God's love, the Christian warrior can overcome and win his way through to heaven, regardless of the contempt or abuse of the world. This triumphant rallying call is not typical of Anne's religious poetry; usually her doubts about her own worth and a deep sense of personal sin put her in the position of an appellant for mercy, seeking salvation as a gift bestowed by God through Christ. In this poem, however, the underlying assumption, which gives such sureness to the vocabulary, is that the man of steadfast and pure intent can earn himself a place in heaven. Charlotte published the poem in 1850, and gave it the title 'The Narrow Way'.

Text: 1850.

87 Last Lines (7—28 January 1849). During the first week of January 1849 Ellen Nussey visited Haworth Parsonage. She found the family 'calm and sustained' in the wake of Emily's death a fortnight before, but anxious about Anne's state of health. The best doctor in Leeds was summoned: 'While consultations were going on in Mr Brontë's study, Anne was very lively in conversation, walking round the room supported by me. Mr Brontë joined us after Mr Teale's departure, and, seating himself on the couch, he drew Anne towards him and said, "My dear little Anne." That was all – but it was understood.' (BST:8:42:21.)

This poem, begun on 7 January, committed to paper Anne's first thoughts on hearing her own death sentence: she could be under no illusions as to the sufferings she would have to endure, for she had watched Branwell and Emily die of the same disease, consumption, in the last four months. On 5 April 1849, she wrote to Ellen Nussey to arrange a sea-cure at Scarborough: her letter reflects the same sentiments as those expressed in her poem: 'I have no horror of death: if I thought it inevitable, I think I could quietly resign myself to the prospect . . . But I wish it would please God to spare me not only for papa's and Charlotte's sakes, but because I long to do some good in the world before I leave it. I have many schemes in my head for future practice, humble and limited indeed, but still I should not like them all to come to nothing and myself to have lived to so little purpose. But God's will be done.' (L. & L., ii, 39.) Anne died on 28 May 1849 at Scarborough and was buried there in St Mary's churchyard overlooking the sea she had always loved.

Eight out of the original seventeen stanzas were published by Charlotte in 1850, thereby removing the stronger expressions of grief, doubt and bewilderment and

creating a false impression of resignation and unfaltering faith which accorded
more exactly with Charlotte's own view of her sister. Her changes in Anne's use
of personal pronouns when addressing God had the effect of reducing the intimacy
of Anne's relationship with God. It has been suggested that the changes in lines
25–8 were made to identify and associate Charlotte with Anne's grief over the
death of Emily, but it seems more likely that 'our delight' and 'our treasured hope'
refer to life rather than to Emily.

1–16 omitted (1850) because they suggest that Anne was not yet fully resigned to
    death.
17 I hoped amid   I hoped that with (1850).
19 labouring throng   busy throng (1850).
20 keen   pure (1850), a variant in Anne's manuscript.
21 But thou   But God (1850).
23 breaking heart   bleeding heart (1850), a variant in Anne's manuscript.
25–8 Thou, God, hast taken our delight
        Our treasured hope away.
        Thou bidst us now weep through the night
        And sorrow through the day. (1850)
29–36 omitted (1850).
38 passive   omitted (1850).
40 Can I but turn to Thee (1850)
41–52 omitted (1850).
54 With   In (1850).
67–8 But Lord! whatever be my fate
        Oh, let me serve Thee now. (1850)

ABBREVIATIONS

1846   *Poems by Currer, Ellis and Acton Bell* (Aylott & Jones, 1846).

1850   *Wuthering Heights, Agnes Grey, together with a selection of Poems by Ellis and Acton Bell* (Smith, Elder, 1850).

BST   *Brontë Society Transactions* (1895 to present day).

Hatfield   *The Complete Poems of Emily Jane Brontë*, ed. C.W. Hatfield
MS   (Columbia University Press, 1941).
L. & L.

The Brontës: Life and Letters, ed. Clement Shorter (Hodder & Stroughton, 1908), 2 vols.

THE BRONTËS AND THEIR CRITICS

When Charlotte was twenty years old and a teacher in her first post at Roe Head, she entertained hopes of becoming a published poet. In order to get an informed and unbiased assessment of her literary talents, she sent a sample of her poetry to Robert Southey, the Poet Laureate. His reply was sufficiently discouraging to prevent her abandoning the safety of her teaching career for the uncertainty of a literary one though she continued to write poetry, as he advised, for 'its own sake'.

Robert Southey to Charlotte Brontë, March 1837.

It is not my advice that you have asked as to the direction of your talents, but my opinion of them; and yet the opinion may be worth little, and the advice much. You evidently possess, and in no inconsiderable degree, what Wordsworth calls the 'faculty of verse.' I am not depreciating it when I say that in these times it is not rare. Many volumes of poems are now published every year without attracting public attention, any one of which, if it had appeared half a century ago, would have obtained a high reputation for its author. Whoever, therefore, is ambitious of distinction in this way ought to be prepared for disappointment.

But it is not with a view to distinction that you should cultivate this talent, if you consult your own happiness. I, who have made literature my profession, and devoted my life to it, and have never for a moment repented of the deliberate choice, think myself, nevertheless, bound in duty to caution every young man who applies as an aspirant to me for encouragement and advice against taking so perilous a course. You will say that a woman has no need of such a caution; there can be no peril in it for her. In a certain sense this is true; but there is a danger of which I would, with all kindness and all earnestness, warn you. The day dreams in which you habitually indulge are likely to induce a distempered state of mind; and, in proportion as all the ordinary uses of the world seem to you flat and unprofitable, you will be unfitted for them without becoming fitted for anything else. Literature cannot be the business of a woman's life, and it ought not to be. The more she is engaged in her proper duties, the less leisure will she have for it, even as an accomplishment and a recreation. To those duties you have not yet been called, and when you are you will be less eager for celebrity. You will not seek in imagination for excitement, of which the vicissitudes of this life, and the anxieties from which you must not hope to be exempted, be your state what it may, will bring with them but too much.

But do not suppose that I disparage the gift which you possess, nor that I would discourage you from exercising it. I only exhort you so to think of it, and so to use it, as to render it conducive to your own permanent good. Write poetry for its own sake; not in a spirit of emulation, and not with a view to celebrity; the less you aim at that the more likely you will be to deserve and finally to obtain it. So written, it is wholesome both for the heart and soul; it may be made the surest means, next to religion, of soothing the mind, and elevating it. You may embody in it your best thoughts and your wisest feelings, and in so doing discipline and strengthen them.

Farewell, madam. It is not because I have forgotten that I was once young myself, that I write to you in this strain; but because I remember it. You will neither doubt my sincerity, nor my goodwill; and, however ill what has here been said may accord with your present views and temper, the longer you live the more reasonable it will appear to you. Though I may be an ungracious adviser, you will allow me, therefore, to subscribe myself, with the best wishes for your happiness here and hereafter, your true friend, Robert Southey.

[L. & L., i, 155–6.]

Branwell's poetry has often been disparaged, mainly because his better poems are not well-known. It would therefore come as a shock to Branwell's critics to learn that Hartley Coleridge, son of Samuel Taylor Coleridge and himself a poet and translator of some distinction, considered Branwell's translations of Horace's *Odes* to be among the best he had ever seen. Branwell met Coleridge briefly at the latter's home on 1 May 1840 while he was a tutor at Broughton-in-Furness. Coleridge evidently praised Branwell's work then and encouraged him to submit further examples of his poems. The irony is that this letter, full of priase which would have meant so much to Branwell, was probably never sent: it exists in draft form only.

Hartley Coleridge to Branwell Brontë, November – December 1840.

Dear Brontë

I fear you have thought me unkind or forgetful in neglecting so long to notice your letter and the enclosed translations. Believe me, I would not be the one, and could not be the other – but I am a sad Procrastinator. I run in debt to Time – and debts of that nature bear compound interest. The longer unpaid – the more difficult to pay. I have however been wiping out a few old scores – this evening – and though I know not whether it be today – or tomorrow – whether Nov 30th or December 1st, I will make an instalment to you forthwith. You are by no means the first or the only person who has applied to me for judgement upon their writings. I smile to think that so small an asteroid as myself should have satellites. But you have heard the distich –

> Fleas that bite little dogs have lesser fleas that bite em –
> The lesser fleas – have fleas still less – so on – ad infinitum.

Howbeit, you are – with one exception – the only young Poet in whom I could find merit enough to comment without flattery – on stuff enough to be worth finding fault with. I think, I told you how much I was struck with the power and energy of the lines you sent before I had the pleasure of seeing you. Your translation of Horace is a work of much greater promise, and though I do not counsel a publication of the whole – I think many odes might appear with very little alteration. Your versification is often masterly – and you have shown skill in great variety of measures – There is a racy english in your language which is rarely to be found even in the original – that is to say – untranslated, and certainly untranslateable effusions of many of our juveniles, which considering how thorough[ly] Latin Horace is in his turns of phrase, and collocation of words – is a proof of sound scholarship – and command of both languages –

[Victor Neufeldt, *The Poems of Patrick Branwell Brontë* (Garland Publishing, 1990), pp.522–3.]

In the 'Biographical Notice' with which Charlotte prefaced the first Smith, Elder & Co. edition of *Wuthering Heights* and *Agnes Grey*, she attempted to dispel some of the wilder rumours and speculation about 'Ellis' and 'Acton Bell'. She publicly revealed for the first time that the two authors were her sisters, now deceased, and sought to portray them as simple unworldly spinsters whose lives had passed in innocent obscurity. In this extract, Charlotte describes the accidental discovery which was to set all three sisters on the path to literary fame.

Charlotte Brontë, Biographical Notice of Ellis and Acton Bell, *1850*.

One day, in the autumn of 1845, I accidentally lighted on a MS. volume of verse in my sister Emily's handwriting. Of course, I was not surprised, knowing that she could and did write verse: I looked it over, and something more than surprise seized me, – a deep conviction that these were not common effusions, nor at all like the poetry women generally write. I thought them condensed and terse, vigorous and genuine. To my ear, they had also a peculiar music – wild, melancholy, and elevating.

My sister Emily was not a person of demonstrative character, nor one on the recesses of whose mind and feelings even those nearest and dearest to her could, with impunity, intrude unlicensed; it took hours to reconcile her to the discovery I had made, and days to persuade her that such poems merited publication. I knew, however, that a mind like hers could not be without some latent spark of honourable ambition, and refused to be discouraged in my attempts to fan that spark to flame.

Meantime, my younger sister quietly produced some of her own compositions, intimating that, since Emily's had given me pleasure, I might like to look at hers. I could not but be a partial judge, yet I thought that these verses, too, had a sweet sincere pathos of their own.

We had very early cherished the dream of one day becoming authors. This dream, never relinquished even when distance divided and absorbing tasks occupied us, now suddenly acquired strength and consistency: it took the character of a resolve. We agreed to arrange a small selection of our poems, and, if possible, get them printed. Averse to personal publicity, we veiled our own names under those of Currer, Ellis, and Acton Bell; the ambiguous choice being dictated by a sort of conscientious scruple at assuming Christian names positively masculine, while we did not like to declare ourselves women, because – without at that time suspecting that our mode of writing and thinking was not what is called 'feminine' – we had a vague impression that authoresses are liable to be looked on with prejudice; we had noticed how critics sometimes use for their chastisement the weapon of personality, and for their reward, a flattery which is not true praise.

The bringing out of our little book was hard work. As was to be expected, neither we nor our poems were at all wanted; but for this we had been prepared at the outset; though inexperienced ourselves, we had read the experience of others. The great puzzle lay in the difficulty of getting answers of any kind from the publishers to whom we applied. Being greatly harassed by this obstacle, I ventured to apply to the Messrs. Chambers of Edinburgh, for a word of advice; *they* may have forgotten the circumstance, but *I* have not, for from them I received a brief and business-like, but civil and sensible reply, on which we acted, and at last made a way.

The book was printed: it is scarcely known, and all of it that merits to be known are the poems of Ellis Bell. The fixed conviction I held, and hold, of the worth of these poems has not indeed received the confirmation of much favourable criticism; but I must retain it notwithstanding.

[Ellis & Acton Bell, *Wuthering Heights & Agnes Grey*
(Smith, Elder & Co., 1850).]

The Brontë sisters' first publication, *Poems* by Currer, Ellis & Acton Bell, received only a few reviews but these were almost uniformly favourable. This first notice was perhaps the least encouraging but it recognised Emily's outstanding talent and quoted from her poem 'The Philosopher' at some length. Charlotte later became friendly with its author, Sydney Dobell, who also favourably reviewed *Wuthering Heights*.

Anonymous Review in the Athenaeum, *4 July 1846.*

The second book on our list furnishes another example of a family in whom appears to run the instinct of song. It is shared, however, by the three brothers – as we suppose them to be – in very unequal proportions;

requiring in the case of Acton Bell, the indulgences of affection . . . and rising, in that of Ellis, into an inspiration, which may yet find an audience in the outer world. A fine quaint spirit has the latter, which may have things to speak that men will be glad to hear, – and an evident power of wing that may reach heights not here attempted.

[Miriam Allot (ed.), *The Brontës: The Critical Heritage* (Routledge & Kegan Paul, 1974), p.61.]

The Brontës were particularly pleased with this review which Charlotte described as 'unexpectedly and generously eulogistic'. It prompted them to expend a further sum of £10 on renewed advertising of *Poems* and they included an extract from the review in all future advertisements.

Anonymous Review in the Critic, 4 July 1846.

No preface introduces these poems to the reader. Who are Currer, Ellis, and Acton Bell, we are nowhere informed. Whether the triumvirate have published in concert, or if their association be the work of an editor, viewing them as kindred spirits, is not recorded. If the poets be of a past or of the present age, if living or dead, whether English or American, where born, or where dwelling, what their ages or station – nay, what their Christian names, the publishers have not thought fit to reveal to the curious reader. Perhaps they desired that the poems should be tried and judged upon their own merits alone, apart from all extraneous circumst-ances, and if such was their intent, they have certainly displayed excellent taste in the selection of compositions that will endure the difficult ordeal.

Indeed, it is long since we have enjoyed a volume of such genuine poetry as this. Amid the heaps of trash and trumpery in the shape of verses, which lumber the table of the literary journalist, this small book of some 170 pages only has come like a ray of sunshine, gladdening the eye with present glory, and the heart with promise of bright hours in store. Here we have good, wholesome, refreshing, vigorous poetry – no sickly affectations, no namby-pamby, no tedious imitations of familiar strains, but original thoughts, expressed in the true language of poetry – not in its cant, as is the custom with mocking-bird poets. The triumvirate have not disdained sometimes to model after great masters, but then they are *in the manner* only, and not servile copies. We see, for instance, here and there traces of an admirer of Wordsworth, and perhaps of Tennyson; but for the most part the three poets are themselves alone; they have chosen subjects that have freshness in them, and their handling is after a fashion of their own. To those whose love of poetry is more a matter of education than of heart, it is probable that these poems may not prove attractive; they too much violate the conventionalities of poetry for such as look only to form, and not to substance; but they in whose hearts are chords strung by nature to sympathize with the beautiful and the true in the world without, and their embodiments by the gifted among their fellow men, will recognize in the compositions of Currer, Ellis and Acton Bell, the presence of more genius than it was supposed this utilitarian age had devoted to the loftier exercises of the intellect.

Being such, we make no apology for extracting from these poems more largely than is our custom, or, rather, than the worthlessness of most of the books of verses submitted to us will permit . . .

[Miriam Allott (ed.), *The Brontës: The Critical Heritage*, pp. 59–60.].

Though published anonymously, the following review of *Poems* was in fact by William Archer Butler, the Professor of Moral Philosophy at Dublin University. The Brontës were so flattered by this favourable notice in a respectable publication that Charlotte wrote personally to the magazine editor to 'thank you in my own name and that of my brothers . . . for the indulgent notice . . . of our first humble efforts in literature'. The reviewer again raised the question which was to haunt all critical notices of the Brontës' works: were the Bells three separate individuals or a single person and were they male or female?

Anonymous Review in the Dublin University Magazine, October 1846.

Of the triad of versemen, who style themselves 'Currer, Ellis and Acton Bell', we know nothing beyond the little volume in which, without preface or comment, they assume the grave simplicity of title, void of *proenomen* or *agnomen* . . . Whether . . . there be indeed 'a man behind' each of these representative titles; or whether it be in truth but one master spirit – for the book is, after all, not beyond the utmost powers of a single human intelligence – that has been pleased to project itself into three imaginary poets, – we are wholly unable to conjecture . . . The tone of all these little poems is certainly uniform; this, however, is no unpardonable offence, if they be, as in truth they are, uniform in a sort of Cowperian amiability and sweetness, no-wise unfragrant to our critical nostrils. The fairest course may, perhaps, be, to present a little specimen from each of the three . . .

Altogether, we are disposed to approve of the efforts of 'these three gentlemen aforesaid' . . . their verses are full of unobtrusive feeling; and their tone of thought seems unaffected and sincere.

[Miriam Allott (ed.), *The Brontës: The Critical Heritage*, pp.63–4.]

In the late summer of 1848, Smith, Elder & Co. purchased the unsold copies of *Poems* from Aylott & Jones and reissued them under their own imprint. This was a matter of relief to the Brontës as they had incurred considerable financial losses when *Poems* was first published. They had had to pay Aylott & Jones not only for the printing and publication costs but also for all the advertising. In this way they had expended some £50 of their very limited capital and, when only two copies were sold, they had no prospect of recovering their money. Smith, Elder & Co.'s reissue therefore offered them a chance to recoup some of their losses. The initial failure, however, left a sense of disillusionment about the book and the poetic talents of the sisters which Charlotte expressed forcibly to the reader at Smith, Elder & Co., her friend, William Smith Williams.

Charlotte Brontë to W.S. Williams, September 1848.

I am glad the little volume of the Bells' poems is likely to get into Mr Smith's hands. I should feel unmixed pleasure in the chance of its being brought under respectable auspices before the public, were Currer Bell's share in its contents absent. Of that portion I am by no means proud. Much of it was written in early youth; I feel it now to be crude and rhapsodical. Ellis Bell's is of a different stamp. Of its startling excellence I am deeply convinced, and have been from the first moment the MS. fell by chance into my hands. The pieces are short, but they are very genuine; they stirred my heart like the sound of a trumpet when I read them alone

and in secret. The deep excitement I felt forced from me the confession of the discovery I had made. I was sternly rated at first for having taken an unwarrantable liberty. This I expected, for Ellis Bell is of no flexible or ordinary materials. But by dint of entreaty and reason I at last wrung out a reluctant consent to have the 'rhymes,' as they were contemptuously termed, published. The author never alludes to them; or, when she does, it is with scorn. But I know no woman that ever lived ever wrote such poetry before. Condensed energy, clearness, finish – strange, strong pathos are their characteristics; utterly different from the weak diffusiveness, the laboured yet most feeble wordiness, which dilute the writings of even very popular poetesses. This is my deliberate and quite impartial opinion, to which I should hold if all the critics in the periodical press held a different one, as I should to the supremacy of Thackeray in fiction. – Believe me, Yours sincerely,
C. Bell.

[L. & L., ii, 256.]

Following swiftly on the heels of the immense success of *Jane Eyre*, Smith, Elder & Co.'s reissue of *Poems* by Currer, Ellis and Acton Bell achieved a much greater level of sales – and attracted more critical attention than its earlier incarnation. It also fuelled the controversy and intense speculation in literary circles about the identity of the mysterious Bells. Despite the different forenames, the critics persisted in believing that the Bells were all one and the same person and applauded their own sagacity in identifying their common traits. With a perspicacity born of hindsight they also, almost uniformly, recognised the greatest talent in the poems ascribed to Currer Bell, ignoring the more obvious merit of both Ellis and Acton's verse.

Anonymous Review in the Spectator, 11 November 1848.

To those who think the subject worth attention, this volume will furnish data for examing the resemblances that have been observed and the differences detected in the prose fictions published separately under the names of Currer, Ellis, and Acton Bell. We do not know that it will settle the question as to whether the writers are identical or merely akin. The mass of the poems in this volume are occasional, and often on such common subjects as are usually found in 'miscellanies': the more peculiar pieces (as far as subject is concerned) are chiefly by Currer Bell, but furnish little means of judging; since all the Bells selected incidents and persons of a singular character, produced by circumstances of a rare kind, or arising from isolated modes of life. In the prose works, the story, however strange and coarse, was consistent with itself and distinct in its purpose. In the larger narrative poems by Currer Bell, both these qualitites are wanting: there is often neither head nor tail; or, when the story is distinctly told, it is not only unlikely, but inconsistent with itself. As far as execution is concerned, the poems under the signature of Currer are entitled to the preëminence. They exhibit more power and possess a greater interest: but this is not conclusive as to difference of authorship. Part of the comparative inferiority of the others may arise from the greater quietness of a small or the triteness of a common subject; it may be accident, or even art.

The essence of poetry – that quality so difficult to define yet so easy to recognise – is rare in the volume. Of the formal and secondary properties there is a good deal. The poems have frequently much strength of thought and vigour of diction, with a manner which, though degenerating into mannerism, is very far removed from commonplace; while in the poorest 'stanzas', without a subject at all, there is still a style which separates them from the effusions of poetasters. The effect of the volume, however, is by no means proportioned to the abilities possessed by the authors. The novels of the Bells have stopped short of an excellence that seemed attainable, from ill-chosen subjects, alike singular and coarse. This defect is visible enough in the poems; but a greater cause of ill success is a disregard of the nature of poetical composition. Where the knack or gift exists, verse can possibly be written with as much certainty as prose, if with less readiness and in less abundance: but the result is the kind of poetry which is not endured by gods, men, or bookstalls. If the structure of the piece does not require more thought than in prose, it requires as much; and, most assuredly, an incident or a narrative that would never be ventured in plain prose, is not from its excess of incongruity adapted to verse. Yet 'Pilate's Wife's Dream,' 'Gilbert,' and perhaps nearly all the story pieces by Currer Bell, are really in this predicament. As regards the sentiments and 'composition' of poetry, there is no doubt but that a careful selection of the thoughts and the exercise of the *labor limæ* are more essential than in prose. Few persons who write down any sudden thoughts that strike them would dream of publishing them in prose; and wherefore in verse? A promising idea rises in the poet's mind, and he commits it to paper; but time is needed to test its value – careful labour to elicit its full proportion, and to clothe it in the most apt language; after all, it may be doomed to the flames, as falling short of necessary excellence. We suspect such kind of care has not been bestowed upon this volume: the indispensable arts of selection and of blotting are yet to be learned by the Bells. If, as seems not unlikely, they are infected with a rage for literary experiment and an itch of writing, they will by no means fulfil the expectation which some have formed of them, or even hold their ground; expecially as their experience or their taste seems limited to one kind of life, and that both peculiar and extreme.

[Miriam Allott (ed.), *The Brontës, The Critical Heritage*, pp.64–6.]

By the time Smith, Elder & Co. had reissued *Poems*, the Bells had achieved an undreamt-of and unwanted notoriety. Their novels had been condemned in many quarters as brutal, coarse and even depraved and the little volume of *Poems* did nothing to redeem the Bells' reputation in the eyes of reviewers such as the one in *Tait's Edinburgh Magazine*.

Review *in* Tait's Edinburgh Magazine, *vol. 15, 1848.*

Poems by the authors of *Jane Eyre, Wuthering Heights* and *The Tenant of Wildfell Hall* are likely to sell, although we should say all manner of evil respecting them.

The three novels acquired a sudden reputation, deserved by *Jane Eyre*, more than by *Wuthering Heights*; and for the other, we have not read the volumes.

The two novels appeared to be written by one hand. *Wuthering Heights* was an exaggeration of *Jane Eyre*, with its blemishes raised, and its virtues depressed.

The little volume of poems bears the impress of one mind. If there have been three of the family engaged on this thin book, they must be marvellously alike.

The poetry is not much liked by us, but we have heard it very greatly praised by others . . .

[Jean-Pierre Petit (ed.), *Emily Brontë* (Penguin Critical Anthologies, Harmondsworth, 1973), p.36.]

Not all reviewers were convinced that Currer, Ellis and Acton Bell were one and the same man; some were perceptive enough to mark the family resemblance in the poetry while still recognising the individual stamp of separate minds.

Review in the Critic, 15 December 1848.

The poetry of Ellis Bell is in general less objective than that of the other two. We say *in general*, for it is in the occasional glimpses in each, of the characteristics of all, that the family likeness . . . in part consists. As a look or a tone in one brother will suddenly recall another, so here will be an expression, a passage, or even the whole tone of a piece in one of these authors, remind us of another, whilst at the same time the individuality of each is strictly preserved. With very few exceptions, the poems of Ellis deal with abstract ideas rather than with actual events. He is the most metaphysical of the three.

[Jean-Pierre Petit (ed.), *Emily Brontë,* p.37.]

Charlotte met Mrs Gaskell for the first time in August 1850 when they were both guests of Sir James Kay-Shuttleworth in the Lake District. The two authoresses immediately became fast friends and exchanged a number of books and letters. Under pressure from Mrs Gaskell, Charlotte reluctantly agreed to send her a copy of *Poems* by Currer, Ellis and Acton Bell though taking care to disparage her own contribution. It is interesting that she here refers contemptuously to the poems as 'rhymes', consciously or unconsciously echoing Emily's description of the book (see p.151).

Charlotte Brontë to Mrs Gaskell, 26 September 1850.

The little book of Rhymes was sent by way of fulfilling a rashly made promise; and the promise was made to prevent you from throwing away four shillings in an injudicious purchase: I do not like my own share of the work, nor care that it should be read. Ellis Bell's poems I think good and vigorous, and Acton's have the merit of truth and simplicity. Mine are chiefly juvenile productions; the restless effervescence of a mind that would not be still. In those days, the sea too often 'wrought and was tempestuous,' and weed, sand, shingle – all turned up in the tumult. This image is much too magnificent for the subject, but you will pardon it.

[L. & L., iii, 162.]

Emily's reputation as a poet and an author began to undergo a major reassessment in the 1870s. After the initial hostile critical response to the savage brutality and degeneracy of *Wuthering Heights*, her novel had sunk into obscurity and remained largely unread. Her poems suffered a similar fate, only arousing curiosity because of her relationship with Charlotte whose fame had continued to grow after the publication of Mrs Gaskell's sympathetic biography. The sudden and unexpected interest in Emily's writings brought a long overdue recognition of her talents, epitomised by this review.

Anonymous article, 'The life and writings of Emily Brontë', in Galaxy, February 1873.

Emily Brontë stands alone among female poets, and, Robert Browning excepted, alone among the English poets of the present century, in the peculiar power, the power of concentrating into a small space a profound psychological study, and a complete history of human life and love, and of expressing it with rare simplicity and strength of diction . . .

From *Wuthering Heights* we turn . . . to the thin volume of poems which is all that remains of the published writings of Ellis Bell . . . here her imagination finds its wings . . . which in a few years would have borne her aloft to the zenith of fame and the full blaze of public approbation. Genius illuminates every page of this little volume, though some of the poems are crude and imperfect; and in others we feel that great ideas have found inadequate expression, and that the authoress when she wrote them had not yet got her wonderful powers sufficiently in hand to be able to manipulate them with ease and grace. Again, several are unequal, being in some passages magnificent, and in others weak and halting. But, taken altogether, many of these poems are beautiful, powerful, and original, so entirely free from the trace of the influence of any other mind upon the mind of the author – the rarest praise that can be awarded to a poet or poetess in these days – that a pang shoots through us as we reflect that we can have nothing more from Emily Brontë's pen. And it provokes a sad smile, too, when we recall the fact that she was so little conscious of the rare beauties contained in this small volume, that it took 'days to persuade her that such poems merited publication.'

[Miriam Allott (ed.), *The Brontës: The Critical Heritage*, p.394.]

By the time Robert Bridges wrote this review of Clement Shorter's edition of *The Complete Poems of Emily Brontë*, Emily's reputation as a writer had undergone a complete revolution. Even so, appreciation of her poetry still lagged far behind the almost universal applause for *Wuthering Heights*. The turn of the century saw a number of Emily's manuscripts made available to the public for the first time and a much wider range of her poetry thus became known. Robert Bridges was in the forefront of the new wave of criticism which was at last to give Emily Brontë due recognition as a poet of outstanding stature.

Reviewed by Robert Bridges in the Times Literary Supplement, *12 January 1911*.

The transcendent genius of Emily Brontë is now well recognised; *Wuthering Heights* has taken its place among the unique creations of literature. But what of the poetess? There is no question of her poetic faculties. The wide intellectual grasp, the unsurpassed power of vivid representation, the almost isolated originality, the concentrated fire of native passion are all undisputed; and yet, with one or two exceptions, her poems – which are her most personal revelation – have made no impression at all . . .

First of all, Emily Brontë is very direct, and eschews ornament. Indeed, it seems probable that what artistic defect her instinct had was indifference to artistic beauty, and that therefore the beauty in her work is that which comes of bare truth and insight rather than of aesthetic handling and ornament. Secondly, she never mastered the technique of poetry, and took what she had chiefly from poets like Cowper. Her biographers, it is true, assert that she was musical; but proficiency in her day, and at a girls' boarding school, implies little; and it would be difficult to find in her writings any evidence of the true musical faculty. In her poems she is certainly not delicately conscious of the music either of her rhythm or of her rhyme . . . Emily has not, therefore, a perfected style. We must not expect either full artistic technique or sustained height of diction; she works without them: and this plainness may deceive; for it is a genius that is speaking, and in her speech the common words have regained their essential and primal significance, and, being the simplest, are therefore for her the best means of direct verbal touch with felt realities.

[Jean-Pierre Petit (ed.), *Emily Brontë*, pp.70–1.]

The critical response to the Brontës' poetry has remained unchanged since the early decades of the twentieth century. Emily is still recognised as the pre-eminent poet of the family but even her work has received comparatively little critical attention, despite the huge volume of criticism generated by *Wuthering Heights*. The Brontës' poetry continues to be treated as a mere adjunct to their novels, worthy of serious consideration only as and when it provides insights into their imaginary worlds, or their own lives. In Charlotte's case this is justifiable as her talents undoubtedly lay in prose writing and her poems were chiefly juvenile productions. Some of Anne's poems, however, including, most notably, 'The Narrow Way', have earned lasting fame by their inclusion in the Methodist hymn-book. Nevertheless, the feminist critics who have done so much in recent years to enhance her reputation as a novelist have largely ignored her poetic output.

The main victim of critical indifference, however, is and always has been, Branwell Brontë. Condemned out of hand by all biographers as a drunkard and a wastrel, it is generally assumed that his poetry was as worthless as the perceived course of his life. This view flies in the face of contemporary opinion, as expressed by numerous eminent writers of the day and confirmed by the number of times his poems found publication in his own lifetime. The Brontë sisters, and most of all their brother Branwell, deserve a major review of their status as poets and a wide-ranging critical appraisal of their poetry is long overdue.

SUGGESTIONS FOR FURTHER READING

Editions

A Funeral Sermon for the Late Reverend William Weightman' by the Reverend
Patrick Brontë (Halifax, J. Walker, 1842).

The Brontës: Life and Letters, ed. Clement Shorter (Hodder & Stoughton,
1908), 2 vols. The first comprehensive edition of the letters of the Brontë family.

The Complete Poems of Anne Brontë, ed. Clement Shorter (Hodder & Stought-
on, 1923).

The Complete Poems of Charlotte Brontë, ed. Clement Shorter (Hodder &
Stoughton, 1923).

The Complete Poems of Emily Jane Brontë, ed. Clement Shorter (Hodder &
Stoughton, 1923).

The Odes of Quintus Horatius Flaccus, translated by Patrick Branwell Brontë,
ed. John Drinkwater (privately printed, 1923).

The Brontës: Their Lives, Friendships and Correspondence, ed. T.J. Wise and J.A.
Symington (Blackwell, 1932, 4 vols.; n.e. 1980, 2 vols.). A revised and expanded
edition of Shorter's Life and Letters.

The Complete Poems of Emily Jane Brontë, ed. C.W. Hatfield (Columbia
University Press, 1941).

Charlotte Brontë: Five Novelettes, ed. Winifred Gérin (Folio Press, 1971). A
selection of five short Angrian stories by Charlotte.

The Poems of Anne Brontë, ed. Edward Chitham (Macmillan, 1979). The most
complete and scholarly edition of Anne's poems.

The Poems of Patrick Branwell Brontë: a new text and commentary, ed. Victor
A. Neufeldt (Garland Publishing, 1990). The best and most reliable complete
edition of Branwell's poems, with comprehensive and scholarly notes.

The Poems of Charlotte Brontë, ed. T. Winnifrith (Blackwell, 1984). A re-issue
of the Charlotte sections of the 1934 Shakespeare Head Brontë edition of The
Poems of Charlotte and Branwell Brontë with variant readings and emenda-
tions recorded in the notes.

The Poems of Charlotte Brontë: a new text and commentary, ed. Victor A.
Neufeldt (Garland Publishing, 1985). An excellent scholarly edition of the
variant texts of Charlotte's poems.

The Juvenilia of Jane Austen and Charlotte Brontë, ed. Frances Beer (Penguin,
1986). A cheap and accessible selection of Charlotte's juvenile writings.

An Edition of the Early Writings of Charlotte Brontë, ed. Christine Alexander
(Blackwell, 1987–92), 2 vols. A comprehensive and scholarly new edition of
Charlotte's juvenile writings.

Emily Jane Brontë: The Complete Poems, ed. Janet Gezari (Penguin, 1992). An
accessible edition of all of Emily's poems.

Biography and Criticism

Mrs Elizabeth Gaskell, *The Life of Charlotte Brontë* (Smith, Elder, 1857), 3 vols. Available in a number of modern editions and the starting point for any study of the lives of the Brontës.

F.H. Grundy, *Pictures of the Past* (Griffith & Farran, 1879). An autobiography by an engineering friend of Branwell's which has some interesting details of Branwell's life.

F.A. Leyland, *The Brontë Family: with Special Reference to Patrick Branwell Brontë* (Hurst & Blackett, 1886), 2 vols. Primarily written as a defence of Branwell by the brother of one of his sculptor friends, who preserved a number of Branwell's letters and poems.

Fannie Ratchford, *The Brontës' Web of Childhood* (Columbia University Press, 1941). An examination and reconstruction of the juvenile writings of the Brontës.

Margaret Lane, *The Brontë Story* (Fontana, 1953). A highly readable biography of the Brontë family, based on Mrs Gaskell but expanded and corrected in the light of modern scholarship.

W.D. Paden, *An Investigation of Gondal* (Bookman Associates, 1958). A reconstruction of Gondal which should be read in conjunction with Ratchford's *Web of Childhood*.

Winifred Gérin, *Anne Brontë: A Biography* (Nelson, 1959).

Winifred Gérin, *Branwell Brontë: A Biography* (Nelson, 1961).

John Lock and W.T. Dixon, *A Man of Sorrow* (Nelson, 1965; repr. Hodgkins, 1979). The best available biography of the Reverend Patrick Brontë.

Winifred Gérin, *Charlotte Brontë: The Evolution of Genius* (Oxford University Press, 1967).

Judith O'Neill (ed.), *Critics on Charlotte and Emily Brontë* (Allen & Unwin, 1968). A fascinating collection of reviews and comments from the Brontës' day onwards.

Winifred Gérin, *Emily Brontë: A Biography* (Oxford University Press, 1971).

Miriam Allot (ed.) *The Brontës: The Critical Heritage* (Routledge & Kegan Paul, 1974). The best and most wide ranging collection of nineteenth-century reviews and criticisms of the Brontë sisters' works.

F.B. Pinion, *A Brontë Companion: Literary Assessment, Background and Reference* (Macmillan, 1975). A useful reference work.

Brian Wilks, *The Brontës* (Hamlyn, 1975). Very readable and superbly illustrated life of the Brontë family.

Christine Alexander, *The Early Writings of Charlotte Brontë* (Blackwell, 1983). A fascinating examination of the complex world of Angria which, of necessity, also covers much of Branwell's juvenilia.

T. Winnifrith and Edward Chitham (eds.), *Brontë Facts and Brontë Problems* (Macmillan, 1983). A collection of essays on a series of interesting problems central to Brontë scholarship.

Valerie Grosvenor Myer, *Charlotte Brontë: Truculent Spirit* (Vision Press, 1987). A stimulating critical interpretation of Charlotte's major novels and useful assessments of past criticism.

Rebecca Fraser, *Charlotte Brontë* (Methuen, 1988). Outstanding as the best modern biography of any of the Brontës.

ACKNOWLEDGEMENTS

I would like to thank the following for permission to use texts: Columbia University Press for C.W. Hatfield's *The Complete Poems of Emily Jane Brontë*; the Council of the Brontë Society for Brontë Society *Transactions*; and the late C.W. Hatfield for his Transcripts in the Brontë Parsonage Museum. I would also like to thank the Council of the Brontë Society for use of the library and archives of the Brontë Parsonage Museum, the staff at the Brontë Parsonage Museum for their suggestions, Sally Johnson for her assistance, Jocelyn Burton of J.M. Dent for her encouragement and support, and finally my husband, whose assistance in this work those who know me will recognise.

*

In preparing this new edition of *The Brontës: Selected Poems* during a period of prolonged ill-health, I have incurred a further set of obligations which I am glad to have the opportunity to acknowledge. First and foremost, my thanks must go to my family, in particular my husband James, my son Edward, my parents Richard and Judith Bateson and my mother-in-law, Shirley Barker. Without their constant cheerful practical aid and moral support daily life – let alone re-editing a book – would have been impossible. I am also grateful to the nurses of the Yorkshire Clinic at Bingley and Mr Mark Pitkethly of the Bradford Palliative Care team for their sympathy and encouragement. Finally, and perhaps most of all, I am indebted to my consultant, Mr Ian Beck, who has looked after me for the past year with exceptional kindness, patience and good-humour; Sophie and I are living proof of his medical skill.

Juliet R.V. Barker, 1993

INDEX OF FIRST LINES

POETRY
IN EVERYMAN

A SELECTION

Silver Poets of the Sixteenth Century

EDITED BY
DOUGLAS BROOKS-DAVIES
A new edition of this famous
Everyman collection **£6.99**

Complete Poems

JOHN DONNE
The father of metaphysical verse in
this highly-acclaimed edition **£4.99**

Complete English Poems, Of Education, Areopagitica

JOHN MILTON
An excellent introduction to
Milton's poetry and prose **£6.99**

Selected Poems

JOHN DRYDEN
A poet's portrait of Restoration
England **£4.99**

Selected Poems

PERCY BYSSHE SHELLEY
'The essential Shelley' in one
volume **£3.50**

Women Romantic Poets 1780-1830: An Anthology

Hidden talent from the Romantic era,
rediscovered for the first time **£5.99**

Poems in Scots and English

ROBERT BURNS
The best of Scotland's greatest lyric
poet **£4.99**

Selected Poems

D. H. LAWRENCE
A newly-edited selection spanning
the whole of Lawrence's literary
career **£4.99**

The Poems

W. B. YEATS
Ireland's greatest lyric poet
surveyed in this ground-breaking
edition **£6.50**

£5.99

£4.99

£3.50

CLASSIC NOVELS
IN EVERYMAN

A SELECTION

The Way of All Flesh
SAMUEL BUTLER
A savagely funny odyssey from joy-less duty to unbridled liberalism **£4.99**

Born in Exile
GEORGE GISSING
A rationalist's progress towards love and compromise in class-ridden Victorian England **£4.99**

David Copperfield
CHARLES DICKENS
One of Dickens' best-loved novels, brimming with humour **£3.99**

The Last Chronicle of Barset
ANTHONY TROLLOPE
Trollope's magnificent conclusion to his Barsetshire novels **£4.99**

He Knew He Was Right
ANTHONY TROLLOPE
Sexual jealousy, money and women's rights within marriage – a novel ahead of its time **£6.99**

Tess of the D'Urbervilles
THOMAS HARDY
The powerful, poetic classic of wronged innocence **£3.99**

Wuthering Heights and Poems
EMILY BRONTE
A powerful work of genius – one of the great masterpieces of literature **£3.50**

Tom Jones
HENRY FIELDING
The wayward adventures of one of literatures most likable heroes **£5.99**

The Master of Ballantrae and Weir of Hermiston
R. L. STEVENSON
Together in one volume, two great novels of high adventure and family conflict **£4.99**

£3.99

£2.99

£3.99

AVAILABILITY

All books are available from your local bookshop or direct from
Littlehampton Book Services Cash Sales, 14 Eldon Way, LinesideEstate, Littlehampton, West Sussex BN17 7HE. PRICES ARE SUBJECT TO CHANGE.

To order any of the books, please enclose a cheque (in £ sterling) made payable to Littlehampton Book Services, or phone your order through with credit card details (Access, Visa or Mastercard) on 0903 721596 (24 hour answering service) stating card number and expiry date. Please add £1.25 for package and postage to the total value of your order.